INTERNATIONAL SEABED AUTHORITY: BASIC TEXTS

Second edition

International Seabed Authority
Kingston, Jamaica, 2012

Published in Jamaica 2012 by
The International Seabed Authority

National Library of Jamaica Cataloguing-in-Publication Data

International Seabed Authority
    International Seabed Authority : basic texts. - 2nd ed.
      p.; cm

    ISBN 978-976-8241-03-0

    1.   International Seabed Authority 2. Maritime Law
    3.   Access to the sea (International Law)
    I.   Title
    341.450262 dc 22

Cover design by Errol Stennett

INTRODUCTION

This second edition of the Compendium of Basic Texts of the International Seabed Authority contains the full text of the rules of procedure of the various organs and bodies of the Authority as well as relevant organizational decisions of those bodies and decisions and documents relating to the external relations of the Authority. The second edition has been updated to include the Supplementary Agreement between the Government of Jamaica and the International Seabed Authority signed in 2003. Since the publication of the first edition, the Authority has further entered into a number of cooperative arrangements with intergovernmental and non-governmental organizations, which are also included in this edition.

The International Seabed Authority came into existence on 16 November 1994, upon the entry into force of the 1982 Convention. In accordance with Part XI of the 1982 Convention and the 1994 Agreement, the Authority is the organization through which States Parties to the Convention organize and control exploration for, and exploitation of, the mineral resources of the deep seabed beyond the limits of national jurisdiction. During the early years of its existence, the efforts of the members of the Authority and the Secretariat were directed primarily towards taking the organizational decisions necessary for the proper functioning of the Authority as an autonomous international organization within the United Nations common system, including election of the various organs and bodies of the Authority, adoption of the rules of procedure for such organs and bodies, adoption of financial regulations, adoption of a Headquarters Agreement and a Protocol on Privileges and Immunities as well as the adoption of the official seal, flag and emblem of the International Seabed Authority. Now that the organizational phase of the Authority is complete, it is useful to present the relevant materials relating to those decisions together in a single volume.

The present volume is designed to complement *The Law of the Sea: Compendium of Basic Documents* published by the Authority in 2001. That volume includes, as well as the full text of the United Nations Convention on the Law of the Sea of 10 December 1982, its nine annexes and associated resolutions, a consolidated version of Part XI of the 1982 Convention and the annex to the Agreement relating to the implementation of Part XI of the United Nations Convention on the Law of the Sea of 10 December 1982 adopted on 28 July 1994 and the Regulations for Prospecting and Exploration for Polymetallic Nodules in the Area, adopted by the Assembly of the Authority in July 2000.

Note on documentary sources

Each section of this Compendium contains a short factual commentary on the origin of the instrument or decision concerned, together with a list of source documents, including relevant working papers and documents of the Preparatory Commission for the International Seabed Authority and the International Tribunal for the Law of the Sea and of the International Seabed Authority.

The documentation of the Preparatory Commission was issued in mimeographed form only (document symbol LOS/PCN/-). However, most of the relevant documents were included in the two final reports of the Preparatory Commission, issued as LOS/PCN/152 (4 vols.) relating to the International Tribunal for the Law of the Sea and LOS/PCN/153 (13 vols.) relating to the International Seabed Authority and the implementation of resolution II of UNCLOS III. The documents for the period 1983-1991, including informal documents, have also been reproduced in systematic form in R. Platzöder (ed.), *The Law of the Sea: Documents 1983-1991* (13 volumes).

The official documents issued by the International Seabed Authority begin with the letters "ISBA". Formal A (Assembly) and C (Council) documents each appear in four series, -/1; -/L.1; -/WP.1; and -/INF.1, corresponding to main documents, documents with limited distribution, working papers and information papers respectively. Documents of the first two sessions do not have a session number (e.g. ISBA/A/1), but from the third session on they do (e.g. ISBA/3/A/1). In addition to A and C documents there are the following series: ISBA/F or FC (Finance Committee) and ISBA/LTC (Legal and Technical Commission).

The International Seabed Authority does not keep verbatim or summary records of meetings. Sound recordings are made and retained by the Secretariat. An account of the meetings of the organs of the International Seabed Authority may be found in the press releases issued by the Authority, but these are not official records and are not necessarily accurate. Official accounts of the work of the International Seabed Authority are to be found in the successive statements of the Presidents of the Assembly and the Council on the work of their organs, and the annual reports of the Secretary-General.

The International Seabed Authority annually publishes a compendium of selected decisions and documents from each session (cited as *Selected Decisions 1/2/3,* etc.). Each volume contains an index to the main documents of the Assembly and Council. Periodically, the *Selected Decisions* contain a cumulative index to those documents.

TABLE OF CONTENTS

I – INTERNAL ORGANIZATION OF THE INTERNATIONAL SEABED AUTHORITY

A – OPERATIONAL RULES OF THE ORGANS OF THE INTERNATIONAL SEABED AUTHORITY

RULES OF PROCEDURE OF THE ASSEMBLY OF THE INTERNATIONAL SEABED AUTHORITY

Table Of Contents

INTRODUCTORY NOTE

On 28 July 1994 the General Assembly of the United Nations adopted the Agreement relating to the implementation of Part XI of the United Nations Convention on the Law of the Sea, and the Agreement has been provisionally applied since 16 November 1994.

According to the Agreement, its provisions and Part XI of the Convention are to be interpreted and applied together as a single instrument; the present rules and references in these rules to the Convention are to be interpreted and applied accordingly.

I. SESSIONS

REGULAR SESSIONS

Regular annual sessions

Rule 1

The Assembly shall meet in regular annual sessions unless it decides otherwise.

Date and duration

Rule 2

The date of commencement and the duration of each such session shall be decided by the previous session of the Assembly.

Notification of members

Rule 3

The Secretary-General shall notify the members of the Assembly at least sixty days in advance of the opening of a regular session.

SPECIAL SESSIONS

Convening of special sessions

Rule 4

1.   The Assembly may convene special sessions and shall fix the date of commencement and the duration of each such session.

2.   At the request of the Council or of a majority of the members of the Authority, the Secretary-General shall convene a special session of the Assembly and it shall meet no earlier than thirty days and no later than ninety days after the receipt of such a request unless the request has stipulated otherwise.

3.   Any member of the Authority may request the Secretary-General to convene a special session of the Assembly. The Secretary-General shall immediately inform the other members of the Authority of the request and inquire whether they concur in it. If within thirty days of the date of communication by the Secretary-General a majority of the members of the Assembly concur in the request, a special session of the Assembly shall be convened by the Secretary- General and it shall meet no earlier than thirty days and no later than ninety days after the receipt of such concurrence.

Notification of members

Rule 5

The Secretary-General shall notify the members of the Assembly at least thirty days in advance of the opening of a special session.

REGULAR AND SPECIAL SESSIONS

Place of meeting

Rule 6

The Assembly shall meet at the seat of the Authority unless it decides otherwise.

Notification to observers

Rule 7

Copies of the notice convening each session of the Assembly shall be addressed to observers referred to in rule 82.

Temporary adjournment of session

Rule 8

The Assembly may decide at any session to adjourn temporarily and resume its meetings at a later date. A regular session shall not normally be adjourned beyond the end of the year.

II. AGENDA

REGULAR SESSIONS

Provisional agenda

Rule 9

The provisional agenda for a regular session shall be drawn up by the Secretary-General and communicated to the members of the Assembly and to observers referred to in rule 82 at least sixty days before the opening of the session.

Drawing up of the provisional agenda

Rule 10

The provisional agenda of a regular session shall include:

(a) The report of the Secretary-General on the work of the Authority;

(b) Reports from the Council and the Enterprise,[1] and special reports requested from the Council or any other organs;

(c) Items the inclusion of which has been ordered by the Assembly at a previous session;

(d) Items proposed by the Council;

(e) Items proposed by any member of the Assembly;

---

[1] See footnote 2.

(f)   Items pertaining to the budget for the next financial period and the report on the accounts for the last financial period;

(g)   Items which the Secretary-General deems it necessary to put before the Assembly.

Supplementary items

Rule 11

Any member of the Assembly, the Council or the Secretary-General may, at least thirty days before the date fixed for the opening of a regular session, request the inclusion of supplementary items in the agenda. Such items shall be placed on a supplementary list, which shall be communicated to the members of the Assembly and to observers referred to in rule 82 at least twenty days before the opening of the session.

Additional items

Rule 12

Additional items of an important and urgent character, proposed for inclusion in the agenda less than thirty days before the opening of a regular session or during a regular session, may be placed on the agenda if the Assembly so decides by a majority of the members of the Assembly present and voting. No additional item may, unless the Assembly decides otherwise by a two-thirds majority of the members of the Assembly present and voting, be considered until seven days have elapsed since it was placed on the agenda.

SPECIAL SESSIONS

Communication of the provisional agenda

Rule 13

The provisional agenda of a special session shall be communicated to the members of the Assembly and to observers referred to in rule 82 at least fourteen days before the opening of the session.

Provisional agenda

Rule 14

The provisional agenda for a special session shall consist only of those items proposed for consideration in the request for the holding of the session.

Supplementary items

Rule 15

Any member of the Assembly, the Council or the Secretary-General may, at least seven days before the date fixed for the opening of a special session, request the inclusion of supplementary items in the agenda. Such items shall be placed on a supplementary list, which shall be communicated to the members of the Assembly and to observers referred to in rule 82 as soon as possible.

Additional items

Rule 16

During a special session, items on the supplementary list and additional items may be added to the agenda by a two-thirds majority of the members of the Assembly present and voting.

REGULAR AND SPECIAL SESSIONS

Explanatory memorandum

Rule 17

Any item proposed for inclusion in the agenda shall be accompanied by an explanatory memorandum and, if possible, by basic documents or by a draft resolution.

Adoption of the agenda

Rule 18

At each session, the provisional agenda and the supplementary list shall be submitted to the Assembly for approval as soon as possible after the opening of the session.

Amendment and deletion of items

Rule 19

Items on the agenda may be amended or deleted by the Assembly by a majority of the members of the Assembly present and voting.

Debate on inclusion of items

Rule 20

Debate on the inclusion of an item in the agenda shall be limited to three representatives of the members of the Assembly in favour of, and three against, the inclusion. The President may limit the time to be allowed to speakers under this rule.

Modification of the allocation of expenses

Rule 21

No proposal for a modification of the allocation of expenses for the time being in force shall be placed on the agenda unless it has been communicated to the members of the Assembly at least ninety days before the opening of the session.

III. REPRESENTATION

Representation

Rule 22

1.   Each member of the Assembly shall be represented by an accredited representative and such alternate representatives and advisers as may be required.

2.   Observers referred to in rule 82 shall be represented by accredited or designated representatives, as the case may be, and by such alternate representatives and advisers as may be required.

3.   The representative may designate an alternate representative or an adviser to act in his capacity.

IV. CREDENTIALS

Submission of credentials

Rule 23

The credentials of representatives and the names of alternate representatives and advisers shall be submitted to the Secretary-General if possible not later than twenty-four hours after the opening of the session. The credentials shall be issued either by the Head of the State or Government, by the Minister for Foreign Affairs or person authorized by him or, in the case of entities referred to in article 305, paragraph 1 (f) of the United Nations Convention on the Law of the Sea, by another competent authority.

Credentials Committee

Rule 24

A Credentials Committee shall be appointed at the beginning of each session. It shall consist of nine members of the Assembly, who shall be appointed by the Assembly on the proposal of the President. The Committee shall elect its own officers. It shall examine the credentials of representatives of members and report to the Assembly without delay.

Provisional admission to a session

Rule 25

Pending a decision of the Assembly upon their credentials, representatives shall be entitled to participate provisionally in the Assembly.

Objection to the representation

Rule 26

If an objection is raised against a representative, such objection shall be considered by the Credentials Committee forthwith. The report thereon shall be submitted to the Assembly without delay for its decision.

V. PRESIDENT AND VICE-PRESIDENTS

Temporary President

Rule 27

At the opening of each regular session of the Assembly, the President of the previous session or, in his absence, the head of the delegation from which the President of the previous session was elected shall preside until the Assembly has elected a President for the session.

Elections

Rule 28

At the beginning of each regular session the Assembly shall elect its President and four Vice-Presidents in such a way as to ensure the representative character of the Bureau. They shall hold office until a new President and other officers are elected at the next regular session.

Acting President

Rule 29

If the President finds it necessary to be absent during a meeting or any part thereof, he shall designate one of the Vice-Presidents to take his place.

Powers of the Acting President

Rule 30

A Vice-President acting as President shall have the same powers and duties as the President.

Replacement of the President

Rule 31

If the President is unable to perform his functions, a new President shall be elected for the unexpired term.

General powers of the President

Rule 32

In addition to exercising the powers conferred upon him elsewhere by these rules, or by the United Nations Convention on the Law of the Sea, the President shall declare the opening and closing of each plenary meeting of the session, direct the discussions in plenary meeting, ensure observance of these rules, accord the right to speak, put questions and announce decisions. He shall rule on points of order and, subject to these rules, shall have complete control of the proceedings at any meeting and over the maintenance of order thereat.

The President may, in the course of the discussion of an item, propose to the Assembly the limitation of the time to be allowed to speakers, the limitation of the number of times each representative may speak, the closure of the list of speakers or the closure of the debate. He may also propose the suspension or the adjournment of the meeting or the adjournment of the debate on the item under discussion.

Limitation of the powers of the President

Rule 33

The President, in the exercise of his functions, remains under the authority of the Assembly.

Voting of the President and Acting President

Rule 34

The President, or a Vice-President acting as President, shall not vote but shall designate another member of his delegation to vote in his place.

VI. BUREAU

Rule 35

The President and Vice-Presidents shall constitute the Bureau which shall meet periodically throughout each session to review the progress of the Assembly and its subsidiary organs and to make recommendations for furthering such progress. It shall also meet at such other times as the President deems necessary or upon the request of any other of its members. The Bureau shall assist the President in the general conduct of the work of the Assembly which falls within the competence of the President. The Chairmen of the subsidiary organs of the Assembly may be invited to attend meetings of the Bureau.

VII. SECRETARIAT

Duties of the Secretary-General

Rule 36

1.   The Secretary-General shall act in that capacity in all meetings of the Assembly and its subsidiary organs. He may designate a member of the Secretariat to act in his place at these meetings. He shall discharge such other responsibilities as are assigned to him by the Assembly in the conduct of its business.

2.   The Secretary-General shall provide and direct the staff required by the Assembly and its subsidiary organs.

Duties of the Secretariat

Rule 37

The Secretariat shall receive, translate, reproduce and distribute documents, reports and resolutions of the Assembly and its subsidiary organs; interpret speeches made at the meetings; prepare and circulate, if so decided by the Assembly in accordance with rule 42, the records of the session; have the custody and proper preservation of the documents in the archives of the Authority; distribute all documents of the Assembly to the members of the Authority and observers referred to in rule 82; and, generally, perform all other work which the Assembly may require.

Report of the Secretary-General on the work of the Authority

Rule 38

The Secretary-General shall make an annual report, and such supplementary reports as are necessary, to the Assembly at its regular session on the work of the Authority. He shall communicate the annual report to the members of the Authority and observers referred to in rule 82 at least forty-five days before the opening of the regular session.

VIII. LANGUAGES

Languages

Rule 39

Arabic, Chinese, English, French, Russian and Spanish shall be the languages of the Assembly and its subsidiary organs.

Interpretation

Rule 40

1.   Speeches made in a language of the Assembly shall be interpreted into the other such languages.

2.   Any representative may make a speech in a language other than a language of the Assembly. In that case he shall himself provide for interpretation into one of the languages of the Assembly. Interpretation into the other languages of the Assembly by the interpreters of the Secretariat may be based on the interpretation given in the first such language.

Languages of resolutions and other documents

Rule 41

All resolutions and other documents shall be published in the languages of the Assembly.

IX. RECORDS

Records and sound recordings of meetings

Rule 42

1. The Assembly may keep summary records of plenary meetings if it so decides. As a general rule, such records shall be circulated as soon as possible, simultaneously in all languages of the Assembly, to all representatives, who shall inform the Secretariat within five working days after the circulation of the summary record of any changes they wish to have made.

2. The Secretariat shall make and retain sound recordings of meetings of the Assembly, and of its subsidiary organs when they so decide.

X. PUBLIC AND PRIVATE MEETINGS OF THE ASSEMBLY AND ITS SUBSIDIARY ORGANS

Public and private meetings

Rule 43

1. The meetings of the Assembly shall be held in public unless the Assembly decides that exceptional circumstances require that the meeting be held in private.

2. As a general rule, meetings of subsidiary organs shall be held in private.

3. All decisions of the Assembly taken at a private meeting shall be announced at an early public meeting of the Assembly. At the close of a private meeting of a subsidiary organ, the Chairman may issue a communiqué through the Secretary-General.

XI. MINUTE OF SILENT PRAYER OR MEDITATION

Invitation to silent prayer or meditation

Rule 44

Immediately after the opening of the first plenary meeting and immediately preceding the closing of the final plenary meeting of each session of the Assembly, the President shall invite the representatives to observe one minute of silence dedicated to prayer or meditation.

XII. PLENARY MEETINGS

CONDUCT OF BUSINESS

Quorum

Rule 45

The President may declare a meeting open and permit the debate to proceed when at least a majority of the members of the Assembly are present.

Speeches

Rule 46

No representative may address the Assembly without having previously obtained the permission of the President. The President shall call upon speakers in the order in which they signify their desire to speak. The President may call a speaker to order if his remarks are not relevant to the subject under discussion.

Precedence

Rule 47

The Chairman of a subsidiary organ may be accorded precedence for the purpose of explaining the conclusions arrived at by that organ.

Statement by the Secretariat

Rule 48

The Secretary-General or a member of the Secretariat designated by him as his representative may at any time make either oral or written statements to the Assembly concerning any question under consideration by it.

Points of order

Rule 49

During the discussion of any matter, a representative of a member of the Assembly may rise to a point of order, and the point of order shall be immediately decided by the President in accordance with these rules of procedure. A representative of a member of the Assembly may appeal against the ruling of the President. The appeal shall be immediately put to the vote, and the President's ruling shall stand unless overruled by a majority of the members of the Assembly present and voting. A representative rising to a point of order may not speak on the substance of the matter under discussion.

Time-limit on speeches

Rule 50

The Assembly may limit the time to be allowed to each speaker and the number of times each representative may speak on any question. Before a decision is taken, two representatives of members of the Assembly may speak in favour of, and two against, a proposal to set such limits. When the debate is limited and a representative exceeds his allotted time, the President shall call him to order without delay.

Closing of list of speakers, right of reply

Rule 51

During the course of the debate, the President may announce the list of speakers and, with the consent of the Assembly, declare the list closed. He may, however, accord the right of reply to any representative if a speech delivered after he has declared the list closed makes this desirable.

Adjournment of debate

Rule 52

During the discussion of any matter, a representative of a member of the Assembly may move the adjournment of the debate on the item under discussion. In addition to the proposer of the motion, two representatives of members of the Assembly may speak in favour of, and two against, the motion, after which the motion shall be immediately put to the vote. The President may limit the time to be allowed to speakers under this rule.

Closure of debate

Rule 53

A representative of a member of the Assembly may at any time move the closure of the debate on the question under discussion, whether or not any other representative has signified his wish to speak. Permission to speak on the motion shall be accorded only to two representatives of members of the Assembly opposing the closure, after which the motion shall be immediately put to the vote. If the Assembly is in favour of the closure, the President shall declare the closure of the debate. The President may limit the time to be allowed to speakers under this rule.

Suspension or adjournment of the meeting

Rule 54

During the discussion of any matter, a representative of a member of the Assembly may move the suspension or the adjournment of the meeting. Such motions shall not be debated, but shall be immediately put to the vote. The President may limit the time to be allowed to the speaker moving the suspension or adjournment of the meeting.

Order of procedural motions

Rule 55

Subject to rule 49, the following motions shall have precedence in the following order over all other proposals or motions before the meeting:
  (a) To suspend the meeting;
  (b) To adjourn the meeting;
  (c) To adjourn the debate on the item under discussion;
  (d) To close the debate on the item under discussion.

Proposals and amendments

Rule 56

Proposals and amendments shall normally be submitted in writing to the Secretary-General, who shall circulate copies to the delegations. As a general rule, no proposal shall be discussed or put to the vote at any meeting of the Assembly unless copies of it have been circulated to all delegations in the languages of the Assembly not later than the day preceding the meeting. The President may, however, permit the discussion and consideration of amendments, or of motions as to procedure, even though such amendments and motions have not been circulated or have only been circulated the same day.

Decisions on competence

Rule 57

Subject to rule 55, any motion calling for a decision on the competence of the Assembly to adopt a proposal submitted to it shall be put to the vote before a vote is taken on the proposal in question.

Withdrawal of motions

Rule 58

A motion may be withdrawn by its proposer at any time before voting on it has commenced, provided that the motion had not been amended. A motion thus withdrawn may be reintroduced by any member.

Reconsideration of proposals

Rule 59

When a proposal has been adopted or rejected, it may not be reconsidered at the same session unless the Assembly, by a two-thirds majority of the members of the Assembly present and voting, so decides. Permission to speak on a motion to reconsider shall be accorded only to two representatives of members of the Assembly opposing the motion, after which it shall be immediately put to the vote.

XIII. DECISION-MAKING

Voting rights

Rule 60

Each member of the Assembly shall have one vote. Participation in decision-making by entities referred to in article 305, paragraph 1 (f), of the United Nations Convention on the Law of the Sea shall be in accordance with Annex IX of the Convention.

Decision-making

Rule 61

1. As a general rule, decision-making in the Assembly should be by consensus.

2. If all efforts to reach a decision by consensus have been exhausted, decisions by voting in the Assembly on questions of procedure shall be taken by a majority of members present and voting, and decisions on questions of substance shall be taken by a two-thirds majority of members present and voting, as provided for in article 159, paragraph 8, of the Convention.

3. Decisions of the Assembly on any matter for which the Council also has competence or on any administrative, budgetary or financial matter shall be based on the recommendations of the Council. If the Assembly does not accept the recommendation of the Council on any matter, it shall return the matter to the Council for further consideration. The Council shall reconsider the matter in the light of the views expressed by the Assembly.

4. Decisions by the Assembly having financial or budgetary implications shall be based on the recommendations of the Finance Committee.

Decisions on amendments to proposals relating to questions of substance

Rule 62

Decisions of the Assembly on amendments to proposals relating to questions of substance, and on parts of such proposals put to the vote separately, shall be made by a two-thirds majority of the members of the Assembly present and voting, provided that such majority includes a majority of the members participating in the session.

Use of terms

Rule 63

1. For the purpose of these rules, the phrase "members of the Assembly present and voting" means members of the Assembly present and casting an affirmative or negative vote. Members of the Assembly who abstain from voting shall be considered as not voting.

2. Subject to the provisions of rules 23 to 26 and without prejudice to the powers and functions of the Credentials Committee, the term "members of the Assembly participating" in relation to any particular session of the Assembly means any member of the Assembly whose representatives have registered with the Secretariat as participating in that session and which has not subsequently notified the Secretariat of its withdrawal from that session or part of it. The Secretariat shall keep a register for this purpose.

Deferment of voting on questions of substance coming up for voting for the first time

Rule 64

When a question of substance comes up for voting for the first time, the President may, and shall, if requested by at least one fifth of the members of the Assembly, defer the issue of taking a vote on that question for a period not exceeding five calendar days. This rule may be applied only once to any question, and shall not be applied so as to defer the question beyond the end of the session.

Deferment of voting upon request for an advisory opinion

Rule 65

Upon a written request addressed to the President and sponsored by at least one fourth of the members of the Assembly for an advisory opinion on the conformity with the United Nations Convention on the Law of the Sea of a proposal before the Assembly on any matter, the Assembly shall request the Seabed Disputes Chamber of the International Tribunal for the Law of the Sea to give an advisory opinion thereon and shall defer voting on that proposal pending receipt of the advisory opinion by the Chamber. If the advisory opinion is not received before the final week of the session in which it is requested, the Assembly shall decide when it will meet to vote upon the deferred proposal.

Method of voting

Rule 66

1.   The Assembly shall, in the absence of mechanical means for voting, vote by show of hands or by standing but a representative of any member of the Assembly may request a roll-call. The roll-call shall be taken in the English alphabetical order of the names of the members of the Assembly participating in that session, beginning with the member whose name is drawn by lot by the President. The name of each member of the Assembly shall be called in any roll-call, and one of its representatives shall reply "yes", "no" or "abstention". The result of the voting shall be inserted in the record in the English alphabetical order of the names of the members.

2.   When the Assembly votes by mechanical means, a non-recorded vote shall replace a vote by show of hands or by standing and a recorded vote shall replace a roll-call vote. A representative of any member of the Assembly may request a recorded vote. In the case of a recorded vote, the Assembly shall, unless a representative of a member of the Assembly requests otherwise, dispense with the procedure of calling out the names of the members; nevertheless, the result of the voting shall be inserted in the record in the same manner as that of a roll-call vote.

Conduct during voting

Rule 67

After the President has announced the commencement of voting, no representative of a member of the Assembly may interrupt the voting, except that representatives of members of the Assembly may interrupt on a point of order in connection with the actual conduct of voting.

Explanation of vote

Rule 68

Representatives of members of the Assembly may make brief statements consisting solely of explanations of their votes before the voting has commenced or after the voting has been completed. The President may limit the time to be allowed for such statements. The representative of a member of the Assembly sponsoring a proposal or motion shall not speak in explanation of vote thereon, except if it has been amended.

Division of proposals and amendments

Rule 69

A representative of a member of the Assembly may move that parts of a proposal or of an amendment should be voted on separately. If objection is made to the request for division, the motion for division shall be voted upon. Permission to speak on the motion for division shall be given only to two speakers in favour and two speakers against. If the motion for division is carried, those parts of the proposal or of the amendment which are approved shall then be put to the vote as a whole. If all operative parts of the proposal or of the amendment have been rejected, the proposal or the amendment shall be considered to have been rejected as a whole.

Order of voting on amendments

Rule 70

When an amendment is moved to a proposal, the amendment shall be voted on first. When two or more amendments are moved to a proposal, the Assembly shall first vote on the amendment furthest removed in substance from the original proposal and then on the amendment next furthest removed therefrom, and so on until all the amendments have been put to the vote. Where, however, the adoption of one amendment necessarily implies the rejection of another amendment, the latter amendment shall not be put to the vote. If one or more amendments are adopted, the amended proposal shall then be voted upon. A motion is considered an amendment to a proposal if it merely adds to, deletes from or revises part of the proposal.

Order of voting on proposals

Rule 71

If two or more proposals relate to the same question, the Assembly shall, unless it decides otherwise, vote on the proposals in the order in which they have been submitted. The Assembly may, after each vote on a proposal, decide whether to vote on the next proposal.

Elections

Rule 72

All elections shall be held by secret ballot.

Restricted balloting for one elective place

Rule 73

1.   When one person or a member of the Assembly is to be elected and no candidate obtains in the first ballot the votes of a majority of the members of the Assembly present and voting, a second ballot restricted to the two candidates obtaining the largest number of votes shall be taken. If in the second ballot the votes are equally divided, the President shall decide between the candidates by drawing lots.

2.   In the case of a tie in the first ballot among more than two candidates obtaining the largest number of votes, a second ballot shall be held. If on that ballot a tie remains among more than two candidates, the number shall be reduced to two by lot and the balloting, restricted to them, shall continue in accordance with the preceding paragraph.

3.   If a two-thirds majority is required, the balloting shall be continued until one candidate secures two thirds of the votes cast; provided that, after the third inconclusive ballot, votes may be cast for any eligible person or member. If three such unrestricted ballots are inconclusive, the next three ballots shall be restricted to the two candidates who obtained the greatest number of votes in the third of the unrestricted ballots, and the following three ballots thereafter shall be unrestricted, and so on until a person or member of the Assembly is elected.

4.   The above provisions of this rule shall not prejudice the application of rules 83, 84 and 96.

Restricted balloting for two or more elective places

Rule 74

When two or more elective places are to be filled at one time under the same conditions, those candidates, not exceeding the number of such places, obtaining in the first ballot the majority required shall be elected. If the number of candidates obtaining such a majority is less than the number of persons or members of the Assembly to be elected, there shall be additional ballots to fill the remaining places, the voting being restricted to the candidates obtaining the greatest number of votes in the previous ballot to a number not more than twice the places remaining to be filled; provided that, after the third inconclusive ballot, votes may be cast for any eligible person or member of the Assembly. If three such unrestricted ballots are inconclusive, the next three ballots shall be restricted to the candidates who obtained the greatest number of votes in the third of the unrestricted ballots, to a number not more than twice the places remaining to be filled, and the following three ballots thereafter shall be unrestricted, and so on until all the places have been filled. The above provisions of this rule shall not prejudice the application of rules 83, 84 and 96.

Equally divided votes on matters other than elections

Rule 75

If a vote is equally divided on matters other than elections, a second vote shall be taken at a subsequent meeting which shall be held within 48 hours of the first vote; and it shall be expressly mentioned in the agenda that a second vote will be taken on the matter in question. If this vote also results in equality, the proposal shall be regarded as rejected.

XIV. SUBSIDIARY ORGANS

Establishment

Rule 76

The Assembly may establish such subsidiary organs as it finds necessary for the exercise of its functions.

Composition

Rule 77

In the composition of subsidiary organs due account shall be taken of the principle of equitable geographical distribution and of special interests and the need for members qualified and competent in the relevant technical questions dealt with by such organs.

Statements by non-members of a subsidiary organ

Rule 78

Any member of the Assembly that is not a member of a subsidiary organ shall have the right to explain its views to that organ when a matter particularly affecting it is under consideration.

Officers, conduct of business and voting

Rule 79

The rules relating to officers, conduct of business and voting of the Assembly apply, *mutatis mutandis*, to the proceedings of subsidiary organs except that the Chairman of a subsidiary organ may exercise the right to vote.

XV. SUSPENSION OF RIGHTS

Suspension of the exercise of voting rights

Rule 80

A member of the Assembly which is in arrears in the payment of its financial contributions to the Authority shall have no vote if the amount of its arrears equals or exceeds the amount of the contributions due from it for the preceding two full years. The Assembly may, nevertheless, permit such a member of the Assembly to vote if it is satisfied that the failure to pay is due to conditions beyond the control of the member.

Suspension of the exercise of rights and privileges of membership

Rule 81

1.   A member of the Authority which has grossly and persistently violated the provisions of Part XI of the United Nations Convention on the Law of the Sea may be suspended from the exercise of the rights and privileges of membership by the Assembly upon the recommendation of the Council.

2.   No action may be taken under paragraph 1 until the Seabed Disputes Chamber of the International Tribunal for the Law of the Sea has found that a member of the Authority has grossly and persistently violated the provisions of Part XI of the Convention.

XVI. OBSERVERS

Rule 82

1.   The following may participate as observers in the Assembly:

(a)   States and entities referred to in article 305 of the United Nations Convention on the Law of the Sea which are not members of the Authority;

(b)   National liberation movements which in their respective regions are recognized by the Organization of African Unity or by the League of Arab States;

(c)   Observers to the Third United Nations Conference on the Law of the Sea who have signed the Final Act and who are not referred to in article 305, paragraph 1 (c), (d), (e) and (f), of the United Nations Convention on the Law of the Sea;

(d)   The United Nations, its specialized agencies, the International Atomic Energy Agency and other intergovernmental organizations invited by the Assembly;

(e)   Non-governmental organizations with which the Secretary-General has entered into arrangements in accordance with article 169, paragraph 1, of the United Nations Convention on the Law of the Sea, and other non-governmental organizations invited by the Assembly which have demonstrated their interest in matters under the consideration by the Assembly.

2. Observers referred to in paragraph 1 (a), (b) and (c) of this rule may participate subject to the provisions of these rules in the deliberations of the Assembly and its subsidiary organs but shall not be entitled to participate in the taking of decisions.

3. Observers referred to in paragraph 1 (d) of this rule may participate in the deliberations of the Assembly upon the invitation of the President on questions within the scope of their competence.

4. Written statements submitted by observers referred to in paragraph 1 (d) of this rule shall be distributed by the Secretariat to the members of the Assembly.

5. Observers referred to in paragraph 1 (e) of this rule may sit at public meetings of the Assembly, and upon the invitation of the President and subject to the approval by the Assembly may make oral statements on questions within the scope of their activities.

6. Written statements submitted by observers referred to in paragraph 1 (e) of this rule within the scope of their activities which are relevant to the work of the Assembly should be made available by the Secretariat in the quantities and in the languages in which the statements are submitted.

XVII. ELECTIONS TO ORGANS

MEMBERS OF THE COUNCIL

Nominations

Rule 83

1. Before electing the members of the Council, the Assembly shall establish lists of countries fulfilling the criteria for membership in the groups of States referred to in rule 84 (a) to (d). If a State fulfils the criteria for membership in more than one group it will be included in the lists of all relevant groups but it may only be proposed by one group for election to the Council and it shall represent only that group in voting in the Council.

2. Each group of States referred to in rule 84 (a) to (d) shall be represented in the Council by those members nominated by that group. Each group shall nominate only as many candidates as the number of seats required to be filled by that group. When the number of potential candidates in each of the groups referred to in rule 84 (a) to (e) exceeds the number of seats available in each of those respective groups, as a general rule, the principle of rotation shall apply. States members of each of those groups shall determine how this principle shall apply in those groups.

Elections

Rule 84

The Council shall consist of 36 members of the Authority elected by the Assembly in the following order:

  (a) Four members from among those States Parties which, during the last five years for which statistics are available, have either consumed more than 2 per cent in value terms of total world consumption or have had net imports of more than 2 per cent in value terms of total world imports of the commodities produced from the categories of minerals to be derived from the Area, provided that the four members shall include one State from the Eastern European region having the largest economy in that region in terms of gross domestic product and the State, on the date of entry into force of the Convention, having the largest economy in terms of gross domestic product, if such States wish to be represented in this group;

  (b) Four members from among the eight States Parties which have made the largest investments in preparation for and in the conduct of activities in the Area, either directly or through their nationals;

  (c) Four members from among States Parties which, on the basis of production in areas under their jurisdiction, are major net exporters of the categories of minerals to be derived from the Area, including at least two developing States whose exports of such minerals have a substantial bearing upon their economies;

  (d) Six members from among developing States Parties, representing special interests. The special interests to be represented shall include those of States with large populations, States which are land-locked or geographically disadvantaged, island States, States which are major importers of the categories of minerals to be derived from the Area, States which are potential producers of such minerals and least developed States;

  (e) Eighteen members elected according to the principle of ensuring an equitable geographical distribution of seats in the Council as a whole, provided that each geographical region shall have at least one member elected under this subparagraph. For this purpose, the geographical regions shall be Africa, Asia, Eastern Europe, Latin America and the Caribbean and Western Europe and Others.

Terms of office

Rule 85

Each member of the Council shall be elected for four years. At the first election, however, the term of one half of the members of each group referred to in rule 84 shall be for two years. Determination of the members whose terms are to expire at the end of two years shall, as a general rule, be left to the agreement of each group. If no agreement can be reached, the members whose terms are to expire at the end of two years shall be chosen by lot to be drawn by the President of the Assembly immediately after the first election.

Eligibility for re-election

Rule 86

Members of the Council shall be eligible for re-election, but due regard should be paid to the desirability of rotation of membership. Members of the Council which were elected upon the nomination by one of the groups referred to in rule 84 (a) to (d) but which fulfil the criteria for membership in other groups, may be re-elected to the Council upon the nomination by one of those groups.

By-elections

Rule 87

Should a member cease to belong to the Council before its term of office expires, a by-election shall be held separately at the next session of the Assembly to elect a member for the unexpired term.

THE SECRETARY-GENERAL OF THE AUTHORITY

Election of the Secretary-General

Rule 88

The Secretary-General shall be elected for four years by the Assembly from among the candidates proposed by the Council and may be re-elected.

THE ENTERPRISE[2]

Elections

Rule 89

1.   The Assembly shall elect, upon the recommendation of the Council, the fifteen members of the Governing Board of the Enterprise.

2.   In the election of the members of the Board, due regard shall be paid to the principle of equitable geographical distribution. In submitting nominations of

---

[2]   According to the Agreement relating to the implementation of Part XI of the United Nations Convention on the Law of the Sea, the Secretariat of the Authority shall perform the functions of the Enterprise until it begins to operate independently of the Secretariat. Upon the approval of a plan of work for exploitation for an entity other than the Enterprise, or upon receipt by the Council of an application for a joint-venture operation with the Enterprise, the Council shall take up the issue of the functioning of the Enterprise independently of the Secretariat of the Authority. If joint-venture operations with the Enterprise accord with sound commercial principles, the Council shall issue a directive pursuant to article 170, paragraph 2, of the Convention providing for such independent functioning.

candidates for election to the Board, members of the Authority shall bear in mind the need to nominate candidates of the highest standard of competence, with qualifications in relevant fields, so as to ensure the viability and success of the Enterprise.

Terms of office

Rule 90

1.   Members of the Board shall be elected for four years and may be re-elected; due regard shall be paid to the principle of rotation of membership.

2.   Members of the Board shall continue in office until their successors are elected.

By-elections

Rule 91

If the office of a member of the Board becomes vacant, the Assembly shall, in accordance with rule 89, elect a new member for the remainder of his predecessor's term.

The Director-General of the Enterprise

Rule 92

The Assembly shall, upon the recommendation of the Council and the nomination of the Governing Board, elect the Director-General of the Enterprise, who shall not be a member of the Board. The Director-General shall hold office for a fixed term, not exceeding five years, and may be re-elected for further terms.

XVIII. ADMINISTRATIVE AND BUDGETARY QUESTIONS

Proposed annual budget

Rule 93

The Assembly shall consider and approve the proposed annual budget of the Authority submitted by the Council taking into account the recommendations of the Finance Committee.

Financial implications of resolutions

Rule 94

No resolution involving expenditure shall be recommended for approval by the Assembly unless it is accompanied by an estimate of expenditures prepared by the Secretary-General and any recommendations of the Finance Committee.

Contributions

Rule 95[3]

The Assembly shall assess the contributions of members of the Authority to the administrative budget of the Authority in accordance with an agreed scale of assessment based upon the scale used for the regular budget of the United Nations until the Authority shall have sufficient income from other sources to meet its administrative expenses.

XIX. FINANCE COMMITTEE

Finance Committee

Rule 96

1.   The Assembly shall elect 15 members of the Finance Committee from the candidates nominated by the States Parties by taking into due account the need for equitable geographical distribution and the representation of special interests. Members of the Finance Committee shall have appropriate qualifications relevant to financial matters.

2.   Candidates for the election to the Finance Committee shall be nominated by the States Parties. They shall be of the highest standards of competence and integrity.

3.   No two members of the Finance Committee shall be nationals of the same State Party.

4.   Each group of States referred to in rule 84 (a) to (d) shall be represented on the Finance Committee by at least one member. Until the Authority has sufficient funds other than assessed contributions to meet its administrative expenses, the membership of the Finance Committee shall include representatives of the five largest financial contributors to the administrative budget of the Authority. Thereafter, the election of one member from each group shall be on the basis of nomination by the members of the respective group, without prejudice to the possibility of further members being elected from each group.

5.   Members of the Finance Committee shall hold office for a term of five years. They shall be eligible for re-election for a further term.

6.   In the event of the death, incapacity or resignation of a member of the Finance Committee prior to the expiration of the term of office, the Assembly shall elect for the remainder of the term a member from the same geographical region or group of States.

---

[3] According to the Agreement relating to the implementation of Part XI of the United Nations Convention on the Law of the Sea, the administrative expenses of the Authority shall be met through the budget of the United Nations until the end of the year following the year during which that Agreement enters into force.

XX. AMENDMENTS

Method of amendment

Rule 97

These rules of procedure may be amended by a decision of the Assembly, taken by a simple majority of the members of the Assembly present and voting, after a committee has considered the proposed amendment.

COMMENTARY

In accordance with its term of reference under Resolution I annexed to the Final Act of the Third United Nations Conference on the Law of the Sea, the Preparatory Commission for the International Seabed Authority and for the International Tribunal for the Law of the Sea had recommended to the Assembly for its consideration draft rules of procedure (LOS/PCN/WP.20/Rev.3). These had been developed by the Preparatory Commission over a number of sessions.

During the second part of its first session, in March 1995, the Assembly of the Authority established a working group consisting of 10 members (two from each regional group) to review the draft rules of procedure. The members of the working group were: Egypt, Brazil, Germany, Indonesia, Jamaica, Poland, Republic of Korea, Russian Federation, Senegal and the United Kingdom. The United States participated in the work of the group as an observer. Mr. Abdoulmagd (Egypt) was elected as chairman of the working group.

In the light of the adoption by the United Nations General Assembly on 28 July 1994 of the Agreement relating to the implementation of Part XI of the United Nations Convention on the Law of the Sea (General Assembly resolution 48/263), the Secretariat had prepared document ISBA/A/WP.1 containing suggestions for revising the draft rules of procedure of the Assembly issued by the Preparatory Commission taking into account the provisions of the Agreement. At the request of the Assembly, the Secretariat then prepared a working paper by merging the two documents. The new document (ISBA/A/WP.2) was then considered by the working group. Following its deliberations, the working group submitted a revision of the draft rules of procedure to the Assembly under symbol ISBA/A/WP.3.

The draft rules were introduced to the Assembly at its fourteenth meeting on 16 March 1995. Following a debate, during which a proposal for certain amendments was submitted by New Zealand (ISBA/A/WP.4), the Assembly adopted its rules of procedure at its fifteenth plenary meeting on 17 March 1995 (ISBA/A/L.2).

DOCUMENTARY SOURCES

- PREPARATORY COMMISSION

LOS/PCN/WP.20/Rev. 3, Final draft rules of procedure of the Assembly of the International Seabed Authority, reproduced in: LOS/PCN/153, Report of the Preparatory Commission under paragraph 11 of resolution I of the Third United Nations Conference on the Law of the Sea, on all matters within its mandate, except as provided in paragraph 10, for presentation to the Assembly of the International Seabed Authority at its first session,[1] Vol. V, p. 3-31.

- ISBA

ISBA/A/2, Draft rules of procedure of the Assembly of the International Seabed Authority.

ISBA/A/6, Rules of procedure of the Assembly of the International Seabed Authority.

ISBA/A/L.1/Rev.1, Statement of the President of the Assembly on the work of the Assembly during the second part of its first session, paras. 4 and 5, (*Selected Decisions 1/2/3*, 4).

ISBA/A/L.2, Rules of procedure of the Assembly. Termination of members of the Council, (*Selected Decisions 1/2/3*, 3).

ISBA/A/WP.1, Suggestions of the Secretariat to revise the draft rules of procedure of the Assembly.

ISBA/A/WP.2, Draft rules of procedure of the Assembly.

ISBA/A/WP.3, Rules of procedure of the Assembly.

ISBA/A/WP.4, Rules of procedure of the Assembly (Proposal submitted by the Delegation of New Zealand).

---

[1] The final report of the Preparatory Commission on matters relating to the International Seabed Authority and Resolution II was issued under symbol LOS/ PCN/153 in 13 volumes. References to that report are in the form LOS/ PCN/ 153, Vol..., p...

OPERATIONAL RULES CONCERNING THE COUNCIL

RULES OF PROCEDURE OF THE COUNCIL OF THE INTERNATIONAL SEABED AUTHORITY

Table Of Contents

INTRODUCTORY NOTE

On 28 July 1994 the General Assembly of the United Nations adopted the Agreement relating to the Implementation of Part XI of the United Nations Convention on the Law of the Sea of 10 December 1982. The Agreement has been provisionally applied since 16 November 1994 and entered into force on 28 July 1996.

According to the Agreement, its provisions and Part XI of the Convention are to be interpreted and applied together as a single instrument; these rules and references in these rules to the Convention are to be interpreted and applied accordingly.

I. SESSIONS

REGULAR SESSIONS

Frequency of sessions

Rule 1

The Council shall meet in regular annual sessions unless it decides otherwise.

Date of commencement and duration

Rule 2

Before the end of each session the Council shall decide on the date of commencement and the approximate duration of the next session.

Notification of members

Rule 3

The Secretary-General shall notify the members of the Council as early as possible but at least thirty days in advance of the opening of a regular session. On the same date he shall notify other members of the Authority.

Alteration of the date of a regular session

Rule 4

1.   Any member of the Council or the Secretary-General may request an alteration of the date of a regular session.

2.   A request coming from a member of the Council shall be submitted to the Secretary-General at least forty-five days before the date originally scheduled and thirty days before the proposed new date. The Secretary-General shall immediately communicate the request to the members of the Council, together with all appropriate observations, including, if any, a statement on financial implications.

3.   A request coming from the Secretary-General shall be subject to the same conditions.

4.   If, within fifteen days of the request, a majority of the members of the Council concurs, the Secretary-General shall convene the session of the Council on the date indicated in the request.

SPECIAL SESSIONS

Convening of special sessions

Rule 5

When the urgent business of the Authority so requires, special sessions of the Council shall be held at the request of:

(a)   The Assembly;

(b)   The Council;

(c)   Any member of the Council supported by a majority of the members of the Council;

(d)   The President of the Council in consultation with the Vice-Presidents of the Council;

(e)   The Secretary-General in consultation with the President of the Council.

Notification of members

Rule 6

The Secretary-General shall notify the members of the Council as early as possible, but no later than twenty-one days in advance of the opening of the special session. On the same date he shall notify other members of the Authority. When a special session is convened to consider an emergency matter under article 162, paragraph 2 (w), of the United Nations Convention on the Law of the Sea, such notification shall be sent as early as possible.

REGULAR AND SPECIAL SESSIONS

Place of meeting

Rule 7

The Council shall meet at the seat of the Authority.

Notification of observers

Rule 8

In accordance with the timetable envisaged in rules 3 and 6, copies of the notice convening each session of the Council shall be addressed to observers referred to in rule 82 of the rules of procedure of the Assembly.

Temporary adjournment of session

Rule 9

The Council may decide to adjourn any session temporarily and resume it at a later date.

II. AGENDA

REGULAR SESSIONS

Drawing up of the provisional agenda

Rule 10

The provisional agenda of a regular session shall include:
(a) Items proposed by the Assembly;
(b) Reports of the Enterprise,[1] reports and proposals of the Economic Planning Commission,[2] the recommendations of the Legal and Technical Commission and reports of the Finance Committee;
(c) Items proposed by the Council;
(d) Items proposed by any member of the Council;
(e) Items proposed by the Secretary-General.

---

[1] According to the Agreement relating to the Implementation of Part XI of the United Nations Convention on the Law of the Sea of 10 December 1982, the Secretariat of the Authority shall perform the functions of the Enterprise until it begins to operate independently of the Secretariat. Upon the approval of a plan of work for exploitation for an entity other than the Enterprise, or upon receipt by the Council of an application for a joint-venture operation with the Enterprise, the Council shall take up the issue of the functioning of the Enterprise independently of the Secretariat of the Authority. If joint-venture operations with the Enterprise accord with sound commercial principles, the Council shall issue a directive pursuant to article 170, paragraph 2, of the Convention providing for such independent functioning.

[2] According to the Agreement relating to the Implementation of Part XI of the United Nations Convention on the Law of the Sea of 10 December 1982, the functions of the Economic Planning Commission shall be performed by the Legal and Technical Commission until such time as the Council decides otherwise or until the approval of the first plan of work for exploitation.

Communication of the provisional agenda

Rule 11

The provisional agenda for a regular session shall be drawn up by the Secretary-General and communicated to the members of the Council and to the members and observers of the Authority as early as possible but at least thirty days before the opening of the session. Any subsequent change in or addition to the provisional agenda shall be brought to the notice of the members and observers of the Authority at least ten days before the opening of the session.

SPECIAL SESSIONS

Drawing up of the provisional agenda

Rule 12

The provisional agenda for a special session shall consist only of those items proposed for consideration in the request for the holding of the session.

Communication of the provisional agenda

Rule 13

The provisional agenda for a special session shall be communicated to the members of the Council as early as possible, but at least twenty-one days before the opening of the session. It shall be communicated to other members and observers of the Authority on the same date. When a special session is convened to consider an emergency matter under article 162, paragraph 2 (w), of the United Nations Convention on the Law of the Sea, the provisional agenda shall be sent as early as possible.

REGULAR AND SPECIAL SESSIONS

Adoption of the agenda

Rule 14

At the beginning of each session, the Council shall adopt its agenda for the session on the basis of the provisional agenda. The Council may, however, in urgent circumstances, make additions to the agenda at any time during a session.

Allocation of items

Rule 15

The Council may allocate items for its consideration or for consideration by any of its organs or any of its subsidiary organs and may refer items without preliminary debate to:

    (a) One or more of its organs or subsidiary organs for examination and report at a subsequent session of the Council;

(b) The Secretary-General for study and report at a subsequent session of the Council; or

(c) The proposer of the item, for further information or documentation.

III. REPRESENTATION AND CREDENTIALS

Composition of delegations

Rule 16

Each member of the Council shall be represented at the meetings of the Council by an accredited representative, who may be accompanied by such alternate representatives and advisers as may be required by the delegation.

Submission of credentials

Rule 17

The credentials of representatives and the names of alternate representatives and advisers shall be submitted to the Secretary-General if possible not later than twenty-four hours after they take their seats on the Council. The credentials shall be issued either by the Head of State or Government, by the Minister for Foreign Affairs or person authorized by him or, in the case of entities referred to in article 305, paragraph 1 (f), of the United Nations Convention on the Law of the Sea, by another competent authority.

Submission of credentials by the members of the Authority not represented on the Council

Rule 18

Any member of the Authority not represented on the Council, attending a meeting of the Council in accordance with rule 74, shall submit credentials for the representative appointed by it for this purpose. The credentials of such a representative shall be communicated to the Secretary-General not less than twenty-four hours before the first meeting which he attends.

Examination of credentials

Rule 19

The credentials of representatives on the Council and of any representative appointed in accordance with rule 18 shall be examined by the Secretary-General, who shall submit a report to the Council for approval.

Provisional admission to the session

Rule 20

Pending the approval of the credentials of a representative on the Council in accordance with rule 19, such representative shall be seated provisionally with the same rights as other representatives.

Objection to representation

Rule 21

Any representative on the Council, to whose credentials objection has been made within the Council, shall continue to sit with the same rights as other representatives until the Council has decided the matter.

IV. OFFICERS

Elections

Rule 22

1.   Each year at its first regular session, the Council shall elect a President and four Vice-Presidents from among its members, so that every regional group is represented by one officer.

2.   In the election of the President the principle of rotation between regional groups shall be observed, and every effort shall be made to elect the President without a vote.

3.   Vice-Presidents shall be eligible for re-election.

Term of office

Rule 23

The President and the Vice-Presidents shall, subject to rule 26, hold office until their successors are elected.

Acting President

Rule 24

1.   If the President finds it necessary to be absent during a meeting or any part thereof, he shall designate one of the Vice-Presidents to take his place.

2.   If the President ceases to hold office pursuant to rule 26, one of the Vice-Presidents shall act in his place until the election of a new President.

Powers of the Acting President

Rule 25

A Vice-President acting as President shall have the same powers and duties as the President.

Replacement of the President or Vice-President

Rule 26

If the President or a Vice-President ceases to be able to carry out his functions or ceases to be a representative of a member of the Council, or if a member of which he is a representative ceases to be a member of the Council, he shall cease to hold such office and a new President or Vice-President shall be elected for the unexpired term.

General powers of the President

Rule 27

In addition to exercising the powers conferred upon him elsewhere in these rules or by the United Nations Convention on the Law of the Sea, the President shall declare the opening and closing of each meeting of the Council, direct the discussions, ensure observance of these rules, accord the right to speak, put questions for decisions and announce decisions. He shall rule on points of order and, subject to these rules, shall have complete control of the proceedings of the Council and over the maintenance of order at its meetings. The President may, in the course of discussion of an item, propose to the Council the limitation of time to be allowed to speakers, the limitation of the number of times each representative may speak on any question, the closure of the list of speakers or the closure of the debate, and the suspension or the adjournment of the meeting or of the debate on the question under discussion.

Functions of the President

Rule 28

1.   The President shall preside over the meetings of the Council and shall represent it in its capacity as the executive organ of the Authority.
2.   The President, in the exercise of his functions, remains under the authority of the Council.

Voting of the President and Acting President

Rule 29

The President, or a Vice-President acting as President, shall not vote, but may designate another member of his delegation to vote in his place.

V. SECRETARIAT

Duties of the Secretary-General

Rule 30

1.   The Secretary-General, as the chief administrative officer of the Authority, shall act in that capacity in all meetings of the Council and of its organs and subsidiary organs. He may designate an officer of the Secretariat to act as his representative. He shall discharge such other responsibilities as are assigned to him under Part XI of the United Nations Convention on the Law of the Sea.

2.   The Secretary-General shall provide and direct, with due regard to the principles of economy and efficiency, the staff required by the Council, its organs and its subsidiary organs.

3.   The Secretary-General shall keep the members of the Council informed of any questions which may be of interest to the Council.

Submission of the annual budget

Rule 31

The Secretary-General shall draft the proposed annual budget of the Authority and submit it together with the recommendations of the Finance Committee to the Council for its consideration. The Council shall consider the proposed annual budget taking into account the recommendations of the Finance Committee and submit it to the Assembly, together with its own recommendations thereon.

Duties of the Secretariat

Rule 32

1.   The Secretariat shall receive, translate, reproduce and distribute documents of the Council and its organs to the members and observers of the Authority; interpret speeches made at the meetings; prepare and circulate, if so decided by the Council in accordance with rule 37, the records of the session; have the custody and proper preservation of the documents in the archives of the Authority; and, generally, perform all other work which the Council may require.

2.   The Secretary-General may distribute to members of the Authority written reports submitted by the non-governmental organizations referred to in article 169, paragraph 1, of the United Nations Convention on the Law of the Sea. Such reports submitted by non-governmental organizations within the scope of their competence which are relevant to the work of the Council shall be distributed by the Secretariat in the quantity and in the languages in which the reports are available.

Estimate of expenditures

Rule 33

1.   Before any proposal which involves expenditures from the Authority's funds is approved by the Council, the Secretary-General shall prepare, as early as possible, a report on the estimated costs involved as well as on administrative and budgetary implications with reference to existing financial authorizations and budgetary appropriations and submit it to the Finance Committee. After consideration by the Finance Committee, the report shall be circulated to all members of the Council together with the recommendations of the Finance Committee thereon.

2.   The Council shall take into account the estimates and recommendations referred to in paragraph 1 before adopting any proposal involving expenditure from the Authority's funds. If the proposal is adopted, the Council shall indicate,

whenever appropriate, the priority or degree of urgency which it attaches to the proposal.

3.   The Council may, in accordance with the procedures established for the operation of a contingency fund to be set up, recommend withdrawals from the contingency fund to meet unanticipated emergencies that may arise before the next regular session of the Assembly.

VI. LANGUAGES

Languages

Rule 34

Arabic, Chinese, English, French, Russian and Spanish shall be the languages of the Council.

Interpretation

Rule 35

1.   Speeches made in a language of the Council shall be interpreted into the other such languages.

2.   Any representative may make a speech in a language other than the language of the Council. In that case, he shall himself provide for interpretation into one of the languages of the Council. Interpretation into the other languages of the Council by the interpreters of the Secretariat may be based on the interpretation given in the first such language.

Languages of resolutions and documents

Rule 36

All resolutions and other documents shall be published in the languages of the Council.

VII. RECORDS

Records and sound recordings of meetings

Rule 37

1.   The Council may decide to keep summary records of plenary meetings; but all decisions taken by the Council and all statements made for the record shall be duly included in the published records of the Council. As a general rule, they shall be circulated as soon as possible, simultaneously in all the languages of the Council, to all representatives, who shall inform the Secretariat within five working days after the circulation of the summary record of any changes they wish to have made.

2.   The Secretariat shall make and retain sound recordings of the meetings of the Council, and of its subsidiary organs when they so decide. The Secretariat

shall provide appropriate facilities to enable members of the Authority to have access to such sound recordings of public meetings upon request.

Communication of decisions

Rule 38

Decisions adopted by the Council shall be communicated by the Secretary-General to the members of the Authority within fifteen days after the close of the session.

VIII. PUBLIC AND PRIVATE MEETINGS OF THE COUNCIL AND ITS SUBSIDIARY ORGANS

Public and private meetings

Rule 39

1.   The meetings of the Council shall be held in public unless otherwise decided.

2.   As a general rule, meetings of subsidiary organs shall be held in private.

3.   All decisions of the Council taken at a private meeting shall be announced at the earliest possible public meeting of the Council. At the close of each private meeting of a subsidiary organ, the Chairman may issue a communiqué through the Secretary-General.

IX. CONDUCT OF BUSINESS

Quorum

Rule 40

A majority of the members of the Council shall constitute a quorum.

Speeches

Rule 41

No representative may address the Council without having previously obtained the permission of the President. The President shall call upon speakers in the order in which they signify their desire to speak. The President may call a speaker to order if his remarks are not relevant to the subject under discussion.

Precedence

Rule 42

The Chairman of an organ of the Council, or of a subsidiary organ of the Council, may be accorded precedence in speaking for the purpose of explaining the conclusion arrived at by that organ.

Statements by the Secretariat

Rule 43

The Secretary-General, or a member of the Secretariat designated by him as his representative, may at any time make either oral or written statements to the Council concerning any question under consideration by it.

Points of order

Rule 44

During the discussion of any matter, a representative of a member of the Council may rise to a point of order, and the point of order shall be immediately decided by the President in accordance with the rules of procedure. A representative of a member of the Council may appeal against the ruling of the President. The appeal shall be immediately put to the vote, and the President's ruling shall stand unless overruled by a majority of the members of the Council present and voting. A representative rising to a point of order may not speak on the substance of the matter under discussion.

Time limit on speeches

Rule 45

The Council may limit the time to be allowed to each speaker and the number of times each representative may speak on any question. Before a decision is taken, two representatives of members of the Council may speak in favour of, and two against, a proposal to set such limits. When the debate is limited and a representative exceeds his allotted time, the President shall call him to order without delay.

Closing of list of speakers, right of reply

Rule 46

During the course of a debate, the President may announce the list of speakers and, with the consent of the Council, declare the list closed. The President may, however, accord the right of reply to any representative if a speech delivered after he has declared the list closed makes this desirable.

Adjournment of debate

Rule 47

During the discussion of any matter, a representative of a member of the Council may move the adjournment of the debate on the item under discussion. In addition to the proposer of the motion, two representatives of members of the Council may speak in favour of, and two against, the motion, after which the motion shall be immediately put to the vote. The President may limit the time to be allowed to speakers under this rule.

Closure of the debate

Rule 48

A representative of a member of the Council may at any time move the closure of the debate on the question under discussion, whether or not any other representative has signified his wish to speak. Permission to speak on the motion shall be accorded only to two representatives of members of the Council opposing the closure, after which the motion shall be immediately put to the vote. If the Council is in favour of the closure, the President shall declare the closure of the debate. The President may limit the time to be allowed to speakers under this rule.

Suspension or adjournment of the meeting

Rule 49

During the discussion of any matter, a representative of a member of the Council may move the suspension or the adjournment of the meeting. Such motions shall not be debated, but shall be immediately put to the vote. The President may limit the time to be allowed to the speaker moving the suspension or adjournment of the meeting.

Order of procedural motions

Rule 50

Subject to rule 44, the following motions shall have precedence in the following order over all other proposals or motions before the meeting:
(a) To suspend the meeting;
(b) To adjourn the meeting;
(c) To adjourn the debate on the item under discussion;
(d) To close the debate on the item under discussion.

Proposals and amendments

Rule 51

Proposals and amendments shall normally be submitted in writing to the Secretary-General, who shall circulate copies to the delegations. As a general rule, no proposal shall be discussed or put to the vote at any meeting of the Council unless copies of it have been circulated to all delegations not later than the day preceding the meeting. The President may, however, permit the discussion and consideration of amendments, or of motions as to procedure, even though such amendments and motions have not been circulated or have only been circulated the same day.

Decision on competence

Rule 52

Subject to rule 50, any motion calling for a decision on the competence of the Council to adopt a proposal submitted to it shall be put to the vote before a vote is taken on the proposal in question.

Withdrawal of proposals and motions

Rule 53

A proposal or a motion may be withdrawn by its proposer at any time before voting on it has commenced, provided that the proposal or motion has not been amended. A proposal or a motion thus withdrawn may be reintroduced by any member.

Reconsideration of proposals

Rule 54

When a proposal has been adopted or rejected, it may not be reconsidered at the same session unless the Council, by a two-thirds majority of the members of the Council present and voting and subject to the requirement referred to in rule 56, paragraph 2, so decides. Permission to speak on a motion to reconsider shall be accorded only to two representatives of members of the Council opposing the motion, after which it shall be immediately put to the vote.

X. DECISION-MAKING

Voting rights

Rule 55

Each member of the Council shall have one vote.

Decision-making

Rule 56

1.   As a general rule, decision-making in the Council should be by consensus.

2.   If all efforts to reach a decision by consensus have been exhausted, decisions by voting in the Council on questions of procedure shall be taken by a majority of members present and voting, and decisions on questions of substance, except where the United Nations Convention on the Law of the Sea provides for decisions by consensus in the Council, shall be taken by a two-thirds majority of members present and voting, provided that such decisions are not opposed by a majority in any one of the chambers referred to in paragraph 5 below. To facilitate the determination of a majority in chambers, ballot papers distributed to the members of each of the chambers should be distinctly marked.

3.   The Council may defer the taking of a decision in order to facilitate further negotiation whenever it appears that all efforts at achieving consensus have not been exhausted.

4.   Decisions by the Council having financial or budgetary implications shall be based on the recommendations of the Finance Committee.

5.   Each group of States elected under paragraphs (a) to (c) of rule 84 of the rules of procedure of the Assembly shall be treated as a chamber for the purposes of voting in the Council. The developing States elected under paragraphs (d) and

(e) of rule 84 of the rules of procedure of the Assembly shall be treated as a single chamber for the purposes of voting in the Council.

Use of terms

Rule 57

1.   For the purposes of these rules, the phrase "members present and voting" means members of the Council present and casting an affirmative or negative vote. Members of the Council who abstain from voting shall be considered as not voting.

2.   Subject to the provisions of rules 16 and 21, the term "members participating" in relation to any particular session of the Council means any member of the Council whose representatives have registered with the Secretariat as participating in that session and which has not subsequently notified the Secretariat of its withdrawal from that session or part of it. The Secretariat shall keep a register for this purpose.

Decisions requiring a consensus

Rule 58

Decisions on questions of substance arising under the following provisions of the United Nations Convention on the Law of the Sea shall be taken by consensus: article 162, paragraph 2 (m) and (o); adoption of amendments to Part XI.

Use of term "consensus"

Rule 59

For the purposes of these rules, "consensus" means the absence of any formal objection.

Method of voting

Rule 60

1.   The Council shall, in the absence of mechanical means for voting, vote by show of hands, but a representative of any member of the Council may request a roll-call. The roll-call shall be taken in the English alphabetical order of the names of the members of the Council participating in that session, beginning with the member of the Council whose name is drawn by lot by the President. The name of each member of the Council shall be called in any roll-call, and one of its representatives shall reply "yes" or "no" or "abstention". The result of the voting shall be inserted in the record in the English alphabetical order of the names of the members of the Council.

2.   When the Council votes by mechanical means, a non-recorded vote shall replace a vote by show of hands and a recorded vote shall replace a roll-call vote. A representative of any member of the Council may request a recorded vote. In the case of a recorded vote, the Council shall, unless a representative of

any member of the Council requests otherwise, dispense with the procedure of calling out the names of the members of the Council; nevertheless, the result of the voting shall be inserted in the record in the same manner as that of a roll-call vote.

Conduct during voting

Rule 61

After the President has announced the beginning of voting, no representative of any member of the Council shall interrupt the voting, except that representatives of members of the Council may interrupt on a point of order in connection with the actual conduct of the voting.

Explanation of vote

Rule 62

Representatives of members of the Council may make brief statements consisting solely of explanations of their votes before the voting has commenced or after the voting has been completed. The President may limit the time to be allowed for such statements. The representative of any member of the Council sponsoring a proposal or motion shall not speak in explanation of vote thereon, unless it has been amended.

Division of proposals and amendments

Rule 63

A representative of a member of the Council may move that parts of a proposal or of an amendment should be voted on separately. If objection is made to the request for division, the motion for division shall be voted upon. Permission to speak on the motion for division shall be given only to two speakers in favour and to two speakers against. If the motion for division is carried, those parts of the proposal or of the amendment which are approved shall then be put to the vote as a whole. If all operative parts of the proposal or of the amendment have been rejected, the proposal or the amendment shall be considered to have been rejected as a whole.

Order of voting on amendments

Rule 64

When an amendment is moved to a proposal, the amendment shall be voted on first. When two or more amendments are moved to a proposal, the Council shall first vote on the amendment furthest removed in substance from the original proposal and then on the amendment next furthest removed therefrom, and so on until all the amendments have been put to the vote. Where, however, the adoption of one amendment necessarily implies the rejection of another amendment, the latter amendment shall not be put to the vote. If one or more amendments are adopted, the amended proposal shall then be voted upon. A motion is considered an amendment to a proposal if it merely adds to, deletes from or revises part of the proposal.

Order of voting on proposals

Rule 65

If two or more proposals relate to the same question, the Council shall, unless it decides otherwise, vote on the proposals in the order in which they have been submitted. The Council may, after each vote on a proposal, decide whether to vote on the next proposal.

Elections

Rule 66

All elections shall be held by secret ballot.

Restricted balloting for one elective place

Rule 67

If, when a person or a member of the Council is to be elected, no candidate obtains in the first ballot the required majority provided for in rule 56, paragraph 2, the balloting shall be continued until one candidate secures the required majority of the votes cast, provided that, after the third inconclusive ballot, votes may be cast for any eligible person or member of the Council. If three such unrestricted ballots are inconclusive, the next three ballots shall be restricted to the two candidates who obtained the greatest number of votes in the third of the unrestricted ballots, and the following three ballots thereafter shall be unrestricted, and so on until a person or member of the Council is elected.

Restricted balloting for two or more elective places

Rule 68

When two or more elective places are to be filled at one time under the same conditions, those candidates, not exceeding the number of such places, obtaining in the first ballot the majority required shall be elected. If the number of candidates obtaining such majority is less than the number of persons or members to be elected, there shall be additional ballots to fill the remaining places, the voting being restricted to the candidates obtaining the greatest number of votes in the previous ballot to a number not more than twice the places remaining to be filled, provided that, after the third inconclusive ballot, votes may be cast for any eligible person or member. If three such unrestricted ballots are inconclusive, the next three ballots shall be restricted to the candidates who obtained the greatest number of votes in the third of the unrestricted ballots, to a number not more than twice the places remaining to be filled, and the following three ballots thereafter shall be unrestricted, and so on until all the places have been filled.

Equally divided votes on matters other than elections

Rule 69

If a vote is equally divided on matters other than elections, a second vote shall be taken at a subsequent meeting which shall be held within forty-eight hours of the first vote, and it shall be expressly mentioned in the agenda that a second vote will be taken on the matter in question. If this vote also results in equality, the proposal shall be regarded as rejected.

XI. SPECIAL PROCEDURES

Approval of plans of work

Rule 70

The Council shall approve a recommendation by the Legal and Technical Commission for approval of a plan of work unless by a two-thirds majority of its members present and voting, including a majority of members present and voting in each of the chambers of the Council, the Council decides to disapprove a plan of work. If the Council does not take a decision on a recommendation for approval of a plan of work within a prescribed period, the recommendation shall be deemed to have been approved by the Council at the end of that period. The prescribed period shall normally be 60 days unless the Council decides to provide for a longer period. If the Commission recommends the disapproval of a plan of work or does not make a recommendation, the Council may nevertheless approve the plan of work in accordance with its rules of procedure for decision-making on questions of substance.

XII. SUBSIDIARY ORGANS

Establishment

Rule 71

The Council may establish, as appropriate, and with due regard to economy and efficiency, such subsidiary organs as it finds necessary for the exercise of its functions.

Composition

Rule 72

In the composition of subsidiary organs, emphasis shall be placed on the need for members qualified and competent in relevant technical matters dealt with by those organs, provided that due account shall be taken of the principle of equitable geographical distribution and of special interests.

Rules of procedure

Rule 73

These rules of procedure of the Council apply, *mutatis mutandis*, to the proceedings of subsidiary organs unless the Council decides otherwise.

XIII. PARTICIPATION BY NON-MEMBERS OF THE COUNCIL

Participation by members of the Authority

Rule 74[3]

Any member of the Authority not represented on the Council may send a representative to attend a meeting of the Council. Such a representative shall be entitled to participate in the deliberations but not to vote.

Participation by observers

Rule 75

Observers referred to in rule 82 of the rules of procedure of the Assembly may designate representatives to participate, without the right to vote, in the deliberations of the Council, upon the invitation of the Council, on questions affecting them or within the scope of their activities.

Cooperation with international and non-governmental organizations

Rule 76

The Secretary-General shall, on matters within the competence of the Authority, make suitable arrangements, with the approval of the Council, for consultation and cooperation with international and non-governmental organizations recognized by the Economic and Social Council of the United Nations.

XIV. ELECTIONS TO THE ECONOMIC PLANNING COMMISSION AND LEGAL AND TECHNICAL COMMISSION[4]

Composition

Rule 77

1.   Each Commission shall be composed of fifteen members, elected by the Council from among the candidates nominated by the members of the Authority.

2.   However, if necessary, the Council may decide to increase the size of either Commission, having due regard to economy and efficiency.

---

[3] This rule is without prejudice to the understanding reached by the Assembly, at the first part of the second session held in March 1996, which provides the following: "The regional group which relinquishes a seat will have the right to designate a member of that group in the Assembly to participate in the deliberations of the Council without the right to vote during the period the regional group relinquishes the seat" (ISBA/A/L.8, note 2, and ISBA/A/L.9, para. 11).

[4] See note 2 above.

3.   In accordance with rule 56, paragraph 2, decisions of the Council on matters referred to in paragraphs 1 and 2 above shall be taken by a two-thirds majority of members present and voting, provided that such decisions are not opposed by a majority in any one of the chambers referred to in rule 56, paragraph 5.

Equitable geographical distribution and the representation of special interests

Rule 78

In the election of members of the Commissions, due account shall be taken of the need for equitable geographical distribution and the representation of special interests.

Nominations

Rule 79

No State Party may nominate more than one candidate for the same Commission. No person shall be elected to serve on more than one Commission.

Term of office

Rule 80

1. Members of the Commissions shall hold office for a term of five years. They shall be eligible for re-election for a further term.

2. A member of a Commission shall begin his term of office on the date of election.

3. In the event of the death, incapacity or resignation of a member of a Commission prior to the expiration of his term of office, the Council shall elect for the remainder of the term, a member from the same geographical region or area of interest.

General qualifications for membership of a Commission

Rule 81

Members of a Commission shall have appropriate qualifications in the area of competence of that Commission. Members of the Authority shall nominate candidates of the highest standards of competence and integrity with qualifications in relevant fields so as to ensure the effective exercise of the functions of the Commissions.

Qualifications for membership of the Economic Planning Commission

Rule 82

Members of the Economic Planning Commission shall have appropriate qualifications, such as those relevant to mining, management of mineral resources activities, international trade or international economics. The Council shall endeavour to ensure that the membership of the Commission reflects all appropriate qualifications. The Commission shall include at least two members from developing States whose exports of the categories of minerals to be derived from the Area have a substantial bearing upon their economies.

Qualifications for membership of the Legal and Technical Commission

Rule 83

Members of the Legal and Technical Commission shall have appropriate qualifications, such as those relevant to exploration for and exploitation and processing of mineral resources, oceanology, protection of the marine environment, or economic or legal matters relating to ocean mining and related fields of expertise. The Council shall endeavour to ensure that the membership of the Commission reflects all appropriate qualifications.

XV. AMENDMENTS

Method of amendment

Rule 84

These rules of procedure may be amended by a decision of the Council, taken by a majority of the members present and voting, after a committee has considered the proposed amendment.

COMMENTARY

As was the case with the rules of procedure of the Assembly, considerable changes were needed in the draft rules of procedure of the Council prepared by the Preparatory Commission (LOS/PCN/WP.31/Rev.3), primarily to take account of the 1994 Agreement. Prior to the second session of the Authority (1996), the Secretariat prepared a further draft of the rules of procedure, taking into account the provisions of the Agreement and the discussions that had taken place with respect to the rules of procedure of the Assembly (ISBA/C/WP.1).

The revised draft was considered in an open-ended working group of the Council chaired by Mr. Marsit (Tunisia). The working group held seven meetings and, at the second session of the Authority, submitted for the consideration of the Council a revised version of the rules of procedure (ISBA/C/WP.1/Rev.1). After consideration of the report of the working group, the Council, at its ninth meeting, on 16 August 1996, formally adopted its rules of procedure (ISBA/C/12).

DOCUMENTARY SOURCES

- PREPARATORY COMMISSION

LOS/PCN/WP.26/Rev.3, Final draft rules of procedure of the Council of the International Seabed Authority, reproduced in: LOS/PCN/153, Vol. V, p. 32-57.

- ISBA

ISBA/A/L.7/Rev.1, Statement of the President on the work of the Assembly during the third part of its first session, para. 34, (*Selected Decisions 1/2/3*, 12).

ISBA/A/L.9, Statement of the President on the work of the Assembly during the first part of the second session, para. 26, (*Selected Decisions 1/2/3*, 21).

ISBA/A/L.13, Statement of the President on the work of the Assembly during the resumed second session, para. 2, (*Selected Decisions 1/2/3*, 29).

ISBA/C/12, Rules of procedure of the Council of the International Seabed Authority.

ISBA/C/L.3, Statement of the President Pro Tem on the work of the Council during the resumed second session, para. 6, (*Selected Decisions 1/2/3*, 39).

ISBA/C/WP.1/Rev.1, Draft rules of procedure of the Council.

DECISION OF THE ASSEMBLY OF THE INTERNATIONAL SEABED AUTHORITY CONCERNING THE DURATION OF TERMS OF OFFICE OF MEMBERS OF THE COUNCIL

The Assembly of the International Seabed Authority,
Decides, in order to harmonize the terms of office of members of the Council with the calendar year, that the terms of office of those members of the Council elected in 1998 will commence on 1 January 1999 and continue for a period of four calendar years and that the terms of office of those members of the Council elected in 1996 for a two-year term will end on 31 December 1998, while the terms of office of those members elected in 1996 for a four-year term will end on 31 December 2000.

53rd meeting
25 March 1998

COMMENTARY

In accordance with paragraph 15, of section 3, of the annex to the 1994 Agreement, the Council shall consist of 36 members of the Authority, elected by the Assembly in the following order:

"(a) Four members from among those States Parties which, during the last five years for which statistics are available, have either consumed more than 2 per cent in value terms of total world consumption or have had net imports of more than 2 per cent in value terms of total world imports of the commodities produced from the categories of minerals to be derived from the Area, provided that the four members shall include one State from the Eastern European region having the largest economy in that region in terms of gross domestic product and the State, on the date of entry into force of the Convention, having the largest economy in terms of gross domestic product, if such States wish to be represented in this group [**Group A**];

"(b) Four members from among the eight States Parties which have made the largest investments in preparation for and in the conduct of activities in the Area, either directly or through their nationals [**Group B**];

"(c) Four members from among States Parties which, on the basis of production in areas under their jurisdiction, are major net exporters of the categories of minerals to be derived from the Area, including at least two developing States whose exports of such minerals have a substantial bearing upon their economies [**Group C**];

"(d) Six members from among developing States Parties, representing special interests. The special interests to be represented shall include those of States with large populations, States which are land-locked or geographically disadvantaged, island States, States which are major importers of the categories of minerals to be derived from the Area, States which are potential producers of such minerals and least developed States [**Group D**];

"(e) Eighteen members elected according to the principle of ensuring an equitable geographical distribution of seats in the Council as a whole, provided that each geographical region shall have at least one member elected under this subparagraph. For this purpose, the geographical regions shall be Africa, Asia, Eastern Europe, Latin America and the Caribbean and the Western Europe and Others [**Group E**]."

The first Council of the Authority was elected on 21 March 1996 (ISBA/A/L.8) following intensive consultations between the regional groups and interest groups. In accordance with the 1982 Convention and the 1994 Agreement, the terms of office of one-half of the members of the Council expired after two years. Accordingly, in March 1998, the first vacancy-filling election was held. At its fifty-third meeting, on 25 March 1998, the Assembly decided that, in order to harmonize the terms of office of the members of the Council to be elected in 1998, their four-year term would commence on 1 January 1999 and continue for a period of four calendar years until 31 December 2002. The Assembly also decided that the terms of office of the members of the Council elected in 1996 for a two-year term would end on 31 December 1998 (ISBA/4/A/5).

Since that time, elections for one-half of the members of the Council have taken place every two years. To facilitate the determination by the Assembly, in accordance with paragraph 9 of section 3 of the annex to the Agreement, of States which would fulfil the criteria for membership in the various groups in the Council, the practice has developed whereby the Secretariat prepares an informal paper containing indicative lists of the States members of the Authority which would fulfil the criteria for membership in the various groups of States in the Council.

DOCUMENTARY SOURCES

- ISBA

ISBA/A/L.1/Rev.1, Statement of the President of the Assembly on the work of the Assembly during the second part of its first session, paras. 7-24, (*Selected Decisions 1/2/3*, 4-7).

ISBA/A/L.7/Rev.1, Statement of the President on the work of the Assembly during the third part of its first session, paras. 4-10, (*Selected Decisions 1/2/3*, 8).

ISBA/A/L.8, Composition of the first Council of the International Seabed Authority, (*Selected Decisions 1/2/3*, 15-17).

ISBA/A/L.9, Statement of the President on the work of the Assembly during the first part of the second session, paras. 2-11 and Annexes I-VII, (*Selected Decisions 1/2/3*, 18-19, 21-25).

ISBA, Indicative list of States which would fulfil the criteria for membership in the various groups of States in the Council of the International Seabed Authority in accordance with paragraph 15 of section 3 of the Annex to the Agreement relating to the implementation of Part XI of the United Nations Convention on the Law of the Sea of 10 December 1982, Informal Working Paper, 27 February 1995. (mimeo.)

ISBA, Alphabetical indicative list of States Members of the International Seabed Authority which would fulfil the criteria for membership in the various groups of States in the Council of the International Seabed Authority in accordance with paragraph 15 of section 3 of the Annex to the Agreement relating to the implementation of Part XI of the United Nations Convention on the Law of the Sea of 10 December 1982, Informal Working Paper 2, 2 March 1995. (mimeo.)

ISBA, Indicative list of States Members of the International Seabed Authority – Potential members of the Groups defined in paragraph 15, subparagraphs (a) through (e) of the Agreement, Informal Working Paper 3, 2 March 1995. (mimeo.)

ISBA/3/A/4, Report of the Secretary-General of the International Seabed Authority under article 166, paragraph 4, of the United Nations Convention on the Law of the Sea, para. 14, (*Selected Decisions 1/2/3*, 48).

ISBA/4/A/5, Decision of the Assembly of the International Seabed Authority concerning the duration of terms of office of members of the Council, (*Selected Decisions 4*, 40).

ISBA/4/A/6, Decision of the Assembly of the International Seabed Authority relating to the election to fill the vacancies on the Council, in accordance with article 161, paragraph 3, of the Convention, (*Selected Decisions 4*, 40).

ISBA/4/A/11, Report of the Secretary-General of the International Seabed Authority under article 166, paragraph 4, of the United Nations Convention on the Law of the Sea, paras. 10-12, (*Selected Decisions 4*, 54).

ISBA/4/A/L.5, Draft decision of the Assembly relating to the election to fill vacancies on the Council.

ISBA, Indicative list of States which would fulfil the criteria for membership in the various groups of States in the Council of the International Seabed Authority during the second 2-year term of the first Council, Informal Working Paper, 16 March 1998. (mimeo.)

ISBA/5/A/7, Decision of the Assembly of the International Seabed Authority relating to the election to fill vacancies on the Council, (*Selected Decisions 5*, 18).

ISBA/5/A/14, Statement of the President on the work of the Assembly at the fifth session, para. 4, (*Selected Decisions 5*, 39-40).

ISBA/6/A/14, Decision of the Assembly of the International Seabed Authority relating to the election to fill the vacancies on the Council, in accordance with article 161, paragraph 3, of the Convention, (*Selected Decisions 6*, 28-30).

ISBA/6/A/19, Statement of the President on the work of the Assembly at its resumed sixth session, para. 14, (*Selected Decisions 6*, 70).

ISBA/6/A/L.3, Draft decision of the Assembly of the International Seabed Authority relating to the election to fill the vacancies on the Council, in accordance with article 161, paragraph 3, of the Convention.

ISBA/6/A/CRP.1, Election to fill the vacancies on the Council for the period 2001 to 2004 in accordance with article 161, paragraph 3, of the Convention, 21 March 2000. (mimeo.)

ISBA/6/A/CRP.2, Indicative list of States Members of the International Seabed Authority which would fulfil the criteria for membership in the various groups of States in the Council, 27 March 2000. (mimeo.)

ISBA/8/A/10, Decision of the Assembly of the International Seabed Authority relating to the election to fill the vacancies on the Council of the Authority, in accordance with article 161, paragraph 3, of the United Nations Convention on the Law of the Sea, (*Selected Decisions 8*, 27-28).

ISBA/8/A/13, Statement of the President on the work of the Assembly at the eighth session, para. 14, (*Selected Decisions 8*, 33).

ISBA/8/A/L.2, Draft decision of the Assembly of the International Seabed Authority relating to the election to fill the vacancies on the Council of the Authority, in accordance with article 161, paragraph 3, of the United Nations Convention on the Law of the Sea.

ISBA/8/A/CRP.1, Election to fill the vacancies on the Council for the period 2003 to 2006 in accordance with article 161, paragraph 3 of the Convention, 19 July 2002. (mimeo.)

ISBA/8/A/CRP.2, Indicative list of States Members of the International Seabed Authority which would fulfil the criteria for membership in the various groups of States in the Council in accordance with paragraph 15 of section 3 of the Annex to the Agreement relating to the implementation of Part XI of the United Nations Convention on the Law of the Sea of 10 December 1982, 19 July 2002. (mimeo.)

ISBA/10/A/12, Statement of the President on the work of the Assembly at the tenth session, paras. 37-38, (*Selected Decisions 10*, 62).

ISBA/10/A/CRP.1, Election to fill vacancies in the Council for the period 2005 to 2008 in accordance with article 161, paragraph 3, of the Convention, 26 March 2004. (mimeo.)

ISBA/10/A/CRP.2, Indicative list of States Members of the International Seabed Authority which would fulfil the criteria for membership in the various groups of States in the Council in accordance with paragraph 15 of section 3 of the Annex to the Agreement relating to the implementation of Part XI of the United Nations Convention on the Law of the Sea of 10 December 1982, 26 March 2004. (mimeo.)

ISBA/10/A/CRP.3, Candidates for election to the Council, 26 March 2004. (mimeo.)

ISBA/12/A/12, Decision of the Assembly of the International Seabed Authority relating to the election to fill the vacancies on the Council of the Authority, in accordance with article 161, paragraph 3, of the United Nations Convention on the Law of the Sea, (*Selected Decisions 12*, 23-24).

ISBA/12/A/13, Statement of the President on the work of the Assembly at the twelfth session, para. 31, (*Selected Decisions 12*, 29-30).

ISBA/12/A/CRP.1, Election to fill vacancies in the Council for the period 2007 to 2010 in accordance with article 161, paragraph 3, of the Convention, 7 August 2006. (mimeo.)

ISBA/12/A/CRP.2, Indicative list of States Members of the International Seabed Authority which would fulfil the criteria for membership in the various groups of States in the Council in accordance with paragraph 15 of section 3 of the Annex to the Agreement relating to the implementation of Part XI of the United Nations Convention on the Law of the Sea of 10 December 1982, 7 August 2006. (mimeo.)

ISBA/14/A/12, Decision of the Assembly of the International Seabed Authority relating to the election to fill the vacancies on the Council of the Authority, in accordance with article 161, paragraph 3, of the United Nations Convention on the Law of the Sea, (*Selected Decisions 14*, 25-26).

ISBA/14/A/13, Statement of the President on the work of the Assembly at the fourteenth session, paras. 19-20 (*Selected Decisions 14*, 29).

ISBA/14/A/CRP.1, Election to fill vacancies in the Council for the period 2009 to 2012 in accordance with article 161, paragraph 3, of the Convention, 21 May 2008. (mimeo.)

ISBA/14/A/CRP.2, Indicative list of States Members of the International Seabed Authority which would fulfil the criteria for membership in the various groups of States in the Council in accordance with paragraph 15 of section 3 of the Annex to the Agreement relating to the implementation of Part XI of the United Nations Convention on the Law of the Sea of 10 December 1982, 21 May 2008. (mimeo.)

ISBA/16/A/11, Decision of the Assembly of the International Seabed Authority relating to the election to fill the vacancies on the Council of the Authority, in accordance with article 161, paragraph 3, of the United Nations Convention on the Law of the Sea, (*Selected Decisions 16*, 34-35).

ISBA/16/A/13, Statement of the President on the work of the Assembly at its sixteenth session, para. 36, (*Selected Decisions 16*, 80).

ISBA/16/A/CRP.1, Election to fill vacancies in the Council for the period 2011 to 2014 in accordance with article 161, paragraph 3, of the Convention, 16 March 2010. (mimeo.)

ISBA/16/A/CRP.2, Indicative list of States Members of the International Seabed Authority which would fulfil the criteria for membership in the various groups of States in the Council in accordance with paragraph 15 of section 3 of the Annex to the Agreement relating to the implementation of Part XI of the United Nations Convention on the Law of the Sea of 10 December 1982, 16 March 2010. (mimeo.)

RULES OF PROCEDURE OF THE FINANCE COMMITTEE

Table Of Contents

INTRODUCTORY NOTE

1.   On 28 July 1994 the General Assembly of the United Nations adopted the Agreement relating to the implementation of Part XI of the United Nations Convention on the Law of the Sea of 10 December 1982, (hereafter referred to as "the Agreement"). The Agreement has been provisionally applied since 16 November 1994 and entered into force on 28 July 1996.

2.   According to the Agreement, its provisions and Part XI of the Convention are to be interpreted and applied together as a single instrument; these rules and references in these rules to the Convention are to be interpreted and applied accordingly.

I. SESSIONS

Frequency of sessions

Rule 1

The Finance Committee (hereafter referred to as "the Committee") shall meet as frequently as required for the efficient exercise of its functions, taking into account the requirement of cost-effectiveness.

Place of sessions

Rule 2

The Committee shall normally meet at the seat of the Authority. Sessions of the Committee may be held at another place in pursuance of a decision of the Assembly or the Council.

Convening of sessions

Rule 3

1.   Taking into account the provisions of rule 1, sessions of the Committee shall be convened at the request of:
   (a)   The Assembly;
   (b)   The Council;
   (c)   The majority of the members of the Committee;
   (d)   The Chairman of the Committee; or
   (e)   The Secretary-General.

2.   Before the Chairman or the Secretary-General make a request to convene a session of the Committee, they shall consult each other and the members of the Committee, including on the date and duration of the session.

3.   Any session of the Committee called pursuant to a request of the Assembly or the Council shall be convened as soon as possible but no later than sixty days from the date of the request.

Notification of members

Rule 4

The Secretary-General shall notify the members of the Committee as early as possible of the date and duration of each session.

Temporary adjournment of session

Rule 5

The Committee may decide to adjourn any session temporarily and resume it at a later date.

II. AGENDA

Drawing up of the provisional agenda

Rule 6

The provisional agenda for each session of the Committee shall be drawn up by the Secretary-General in consultation with the Chairman of the Committee, whenever possible, and shall include:

(a) All items proposed by the Assembly;

(b) All items proposed by the Council;

(c) All items proposed by the Committee;

(d) All items proposed by the Chairman;

(e) All items proposed by any member of the Committee;

(f) All items proposed by the Secretary-General.

Communication of the provisional agenda

Rule 7

The provisional agenda for each session of the Committee shall be communicated to the members of the Committee and the members of the Authority as early as possible in advance of the session, but at least twenty-one days before the opening of the session. Any subsequent change in or addition to the provisional agenda shall be brought to the notice of the members of the Committee and the members of the Authority sufficiently in advance of the session.

Adoption of the agenda

Rule 8

1. At the beginning of each session the Committee shall adopt its agenda for the session, on the basis of the provisional agenda.

2. The Committee may, if necessary, amend the agenda, provided that no item referred to it by the Assembly or the Council be deleted or modified.

III. ELECTIONS AND FUNCTIONS OF THE COMMITTEE

Elections

Rule 9

The members of the Committee shall be elected by the Assembly in accordance with the Convention and the Agreement and the rules of procedure of the Assembly.

Incompatible activities and confidentiality

Rule 10

Members of the Committee shall have no financial interest in any activity relating to matters upon which the Committee has the responsibility to make recommendations. They shall not disclose, even after termination of their functions, any confidential information coming to their knowledge by reason of their duties for the Authority.

Functions

Rule 11

The Committee shall assist the Assembly and the Council in the financial administration of the Authority by providing advice on matters which have financial or budgetary implications and shall, *inter alia*, submit recommendations regarding the following issues:

    (a) Draft financial rules, regulations and procedures of the organs of the Authority and the financial management and internal financial administration of the Authority;

    (b) Assessment of contributions of members to the administrative budget of the Authority in accordance with article 160, paragraph 2 (e), of the Convention;

    (c) All relevant financial matters, including the proposed annual budget prepared by the Secretary-General of the Authority in accordance with article 172 of the Convention and the financial aspects of the implementation of the programmes of work of the Secretariat;

    (d) The administrative budget;

    (e) Financial obligations of States Parties arising from the implementation of the Agreement and Part XI of the Convention as well as the administrative and budgetary implications of proposals and recommendations involving expenditure from the funds of the Authority;

    (f) Rules, regulations and procedures on the equitable sharing of financial and other economic benefits derived from activities in the Area and the decisions to be made thereon.

IV. OFFICERS

Election and term of Chairman and Vice-Chairman

Rule 12

1.   Each year at its first meeting, the Committee shall elect a Chairman and a Vice-Chairman from among its members.

2.   The Chairman and the Vice-Chairman shall be elected for a term of one year. They shall hold office until their successors are elected. They shall be eligible for re-election.

Acting Chairman

Rule 13

1.   In the absence of the Chairman, the Vice-Chairman shall take his or her place.

2.   If the Chairman ceases to hold office pursuant to rule 17, the Vice-Chairman shall take his or her place until the election of a new Chairman.

Powers of the Acting Chairman

Rule 14

A Vice-Chairman acting as Chairman shall have the same powers and duties as the Chairman.

Rapporteur

Rule 15

The Committee may appoint, if necessary, one of its members as Rapporteur for any particular question.

General powers of the Chairman

Rule 16

1.   The Chairman, in the exercise of his or her functions, remains under the authority of the Committee.

2.   In addition to exercising the powers conferred upon him or her elsewhere in these rules, the Chairman shall declare the opening and closing of each meeting of the Committee, direct the discussions, ensure observance of these rules, accord the right to speak, put questions to the vote and announce decisions. He or she shall rule on points of order and, subject to these rules, shall have complete control of the proceedings of the Committee and over the maintenance of order at its meetings. The Chairman may, in the course of the discussion of an item, propose to the Committee the limitation of time to be allowed to speakers, the limitation of the number of times each member may speak on any question, the closure of the list of speakers or the closure of the debate. He or she may also propose the suspension or the adjournment of the meeting or of the debate on the question under discussion.

3.   The Chairman shall represent the Committee at meetings of the Assembly and the Council.

Replacement of the Chairman or the Vice-Chairman

Rule 17

If the Chairman or the Vice-Chairman ceases to be able to carry out his or her functions or ceases to be a member of the Committee, he or she shall cease to hold such office and a new Chairman or Vice-Chairman shall be elected for the unexpired term.

V. SECRETARIAT

Duties of the Secretary-General

Rule 18

1.   The Secretary-General shall act in that capacity in all meetings of the Committee. He or she may designate a member of the Secretariat to act as his or her representative. He or she shall perform such other functions as are assigned to him or her by the Committee.

2.   The Secretary-General shall provide and direct the staff required by the Committee, taking into account to the greatest extent possible the requirements of economy and efficiency, and be responsible for all the arrangements that may be necessary for its meetings.

3.   The Secretary-General shall keep the members of the Committee informed of any questions that may be brought before it for consideration.

4.   The Secretary-General shall provide to the Committee, at its request, information and reports on questions specified by the Committee.

Duties of the Secretariat

Rule 19

The Secretariat shall receive, translate, reproduce and distribute recommendations, reports and other documents of the Committee, interpret speeches made at meetings, prepare and circulate, when it is so decided, records of the session, have custody and proper preservation of the documents in the archives of the Committee, and, generally, perform all other work which the Committee may require.

VI. CONDUCT OF BUSINESS

Conduct of business

Rule 20

As far as conduct of business is concerned, the proceedings of the Committee shall be governed by general practice as reflected in section XII of the rules of procedure of the Assembly.

VII. DECISION-MAKING

Voting rights

Rule 21

Each member of the Committee, including the Chairman, shall have one vote.

Decision-making

Rule 22

1.   As a general rule, decision-making in the Committee should be by consensus. If all efforts to reach a decision by consensus have been exhausted, decisions by voting on questions of procedure shall be taken by a majority of members present and voting.

2.   Decisions on questions of substance shall be taken by consensus.

Meaning of the phrase "members present and voting"

Rule 23

For the purposes of these rules, the phrase "members present and voting" means members present and casting an affirmative or negative vote. Members who abstain from voting shall be considered as not voting.

Conduct of voting

Rule 24

The Committee shall apply *mutatis mutandis* the rules relating to the conduct of voting in rules 66 to 71 of the rules of procedure of the Assembly.

Elections

Rule 25

All elections in the Committee shall be held by secret ballot.

Conduct of elections

Rule 26

The Committee shall apply *mutatis mutandis* the rules relating to elections in rules 73 to 75 of the rules of procedure of the Assembly.

VIII. LANGUAGES

Languages of the Committee

Rule 27

Arabic, Chinese, English, French, Russian and Spanish shall be the languages of the Committee.

Interpretation

Rule 28

Speeches made in any of the six languages of the Committee shall be interpreted into the other five languages.

Other languages

Rule 29

Any member may make a speech in a language other than the languages of the Committee. In this case, he or she shall himself or herself provide for interpretation into one of the languages of the Committee. Interpretation into the other languages of the Committee by the interpreters of the Secretariat may be based on the interpretation given in the first such language.

Languages of recommendations and documents

Rule 30

All recommendations and other documents of the Committee shall be published in the languages of the Committee.

IX. MEETINGS

Private and public meetings

Rule 31

1.   The meetings of the Committee shall be held in private unless the Committee decides otherwise.

2.   At the close of a private meeting of the Committee, the Chairman may, if the Committee so decides, issue a communiqué through the Secretary-General.

COMMENTARY

Although the Preparatory Commission had drawn up draft rules of procedure for a Finance Committee (LOS/PCN/WP.45/Rev.2), these predated the 1994 Agreement and therefore needed substantial revision. Following the election of the first Finance Committee in 1996, a revised draft was prepared by the Secretariat (ISBA/4/F/WP.1 and ISBA/4/FC/WP.2). These were considered by the Finance Committee at its meetings during the third session of the Authority (1997), fourth session (1998) and fifth session (1999). The Committee adopted its rules of procedure on 20 August 1999.

DOCUMENTARY SOURCES

- PREPARATORY COMMISSION

LOS/PCN/WP.45/Rev.2, The Finance Committee, reproduced in: LOS/PCN/153, Vol. V, p. 92-96.

- ISBA

ISBA/4/A/11, Report of the Secretary-General of the International Seabed Authority under article 166, paragraph 4, of the United Nations Convention on the Law of the Sea, para. 57, (*Selected Decisions 4*, 62).

ISBA/5/A/1 and Corr. 1, Report of the Secretary-General of the International Seabed Authority under article 166, paragraph 4, of the United Nations Convention on the Law of the Sea, para. 52, (*Selected Decisions 5*, 11).

ISBA/5/A/8-ISBA/5/C/7, Proposed budget of the International Seabed Authority for 2000 and related matters. Report of the Finance Committee, para. 10, (*Selected Decisions 5*, 20).

ISBA/F/WP.1, Draft rules of procedure of the Finance Committee.

ISBA/4/FC/WP.2, Draft rules of procedure of the Finance Committee.

ISBA/5/FC/1, Rules of procedure of the Finance Committee.

OPERATIONAL RULES CONCERNING THE LEGAL AND TECHNICAL COMMISSION

RULES OF PROCEDURE OF THE LEGAL AND TECHNICAL COMMISSION

Table Of Contents

INTRODUCTORY NOTE

1.   On 28 July 1994, the General Assembly of the United Nations adopted the Agreement relating to the Implementation of Part XI of the United Nations Convention on the Law of the Sea of 10 December 1982 (hereafter referred to as "the Agreement"). The Agreement has been provisionally applied since 16 November 1994 and entered into force on 28 July 1996.

2.   According to the Agreement, its provisions and Part XI of the United Nations Convention of the Law of the Sea of 10 December 1982 (hereinafter referred to as "the Convention") are to be interpreted and applied together as a single instrument; the present rules and references in the rules to the Convention are to be interpreted and applied accordingly.

3.   The Legal and Technical Commission, established under article 163 of the Convention, shall function in accordance with the provisions of the Convention and the Agreement.

I. SESSIONS

Rule 1

Frequency of sessions

The Legal and Technical Commission (hereinafter referred to as "the Commission") shall meet as often as required, including in emergency sessions, for the efficient exercise of its functions, taking into account the requirement of cost-effectiveness.

Rule 2

Place of sessions

The Commission shall normally meet at the seat of the Authority. Whenever circumstances warrant or the business of the Commission so requires, the Commission may, in consultation with the Secretary-General, and taking into account section 1, paragraph 2 of the annex to the Agreement, decide to meet elsewhere.

Rule 3

Convening of sessions

Taking into account the provisions of rule 1, the Commission shall be convened at the request of:

(a) The Council;
(b) A majority of the members of the Commission;
(c) The Chairman of the Commission; or
(d) The Secretary-General.

Rule 4

Notification of the members

The Secretary-General shall notify the members of the Commission and the members of the Authority as early as possible of the date and duration of each session, and shall seek confirmation of their attendance.

Rule 5

Temporary adjournment of session

The Commission may decide to adjourn any session temporarily and resume it at a later date.

Rule 6

Meetings

The meetings of the Commission shall be held in private unless the Commission decides otherwise. The Commission shall take into account the desirability of holding open meetings when issues of general interest to members of the Authority, which do not involve the discussion of confidential information, are being discussed.

II. AGENDA

Rule 7
Communication of the provisional agenda

The provisional agenda for each session of the Commission shall be drawn up by the Secretary-General and communicated to the members of the Commission and the members of the Authority as early as possible but at least thirty days before the opening of the session. Any subsequent change in or addition to the provisional agenda shall be brought to the notice of the members of the Commission and to the members of the Authority sufficiently in advance of the session.

Rule 8
Drawing up of the provisional agenda

The provisional agenda of each session shall consist of:
(a) All items proposed by the Council;
(b) All items proposed by the Commission;
(c) All items proposed by the Chairman of the Commission;
(d) All items proposed by any member of the Commission;
(e) All items proposed by the Secretary-General.

Rule 9
Adoption of the agenda

At the beginning of each session, the Commission shall adopt its agenda for the session on the basis of the provisional agenda. The Commission may, if necessary, amend the agenda at any time during a session.

III. ELECTIONS AND FUNCTIONS

Rule 10
Elections

The members of the Commission shall be elected by the Council in accordance with the Convention and the rules of procedure of the Council.

Rule 11
Conflict of interest

1.   Members of the Commission shall have no financial interest in any activity relating to exploration and exploitation in the Area.

2.   Before assuming his or her duties, each member of the Commission shall make the following written declaration witnessed by the Secretary-General or his authorized representative:

> "I solemnly declare that I will perform my duties as a
> member of the Legal and Technical Commission, honourably,
> faithfully, impartially and conscientiously.

"I further solemnly declare and promise that I shall have no financial interest in any activity relating to exploration and exploitation in the Area. Subject to my responsibilities to the Legal and Technical Commission, I shall not disclose, even after the termination of my functions, any industrial secret, proprietary data which are transferred to the Authority in accordance with the Convention and the Agreement, or any other confidential information coming to my knowledge by reason of my duties for the Authority.

"I shall disclose to the Secretary-General and to the Commission any interest in any matter under discussion before the Commission which might constitute a conflict of interest or which might be incompatible with the requirements of integrity and impartiality expected of a member of the Commission and I shall refrain from participating in the work of the Commission in relation to such matter."

Rule 12
Confidentiality

1.   Subject to their responsibilities to the Commission, members of the Commission shall not disclose, even after the termination of their functions, any industrial secret, proprietary data which are transferred to the Authority in accordance with annex III, article 14, of the Convention, or any other confidential information coming to their knowledge by reason of their duties for the Authority.

2.   The Commission shall recommend to the Council, for approval, procedures on the handling of confidential data and information coming to the knowledge of members of the Commission by reason of their duties for the Commission. Such procedures shall be based upon the relevant provisions of the Convention, the rules, regulations and procedures of the Authority and the procedures established by the Secretary-General pursuant thereto in order to carry out his responsibility to maintain the confidentiality of such data and information.

3.   The duty of the members of the Commission not to disclose confidential information constitutes an obligation in respect of that member and shall remain an obligation after the expiration or termination of that member's functions for the Commission.

Rule 13
Enforcement of rules relating to conflict of interest and confidentiality

1.   The Secretary-General shall provide the Commission and the Council with all necessary assistance in enforcing the rules on conflict of interest and confidentiality.

2.   In the event of an alleged breach of the obligations relating to conflict of interest and confidentiality by a member of the Commission, the Council may institute appropriate proceedings and shall make known its findings and recommendations.

Rule 14
Exercise of functions

The Commission shall exercise its functions in accordance with these Rules and such guidelines as the Council may adopt from time to time.

Rule 15
Consultations

In the exercise of its functions, the Commission may, where appropriate, consult another commission, any competent organ of the United Nations or of its specialized agencies or any international organizations with competence in the subject-matter of such consultation.

IV. OFFICERS

Rule 16
Election and term of Chairman

1. Each year at the first session, the Commission shall elect a Chairman and a Vice-Chairman from among its members.
2. The Chairman and the Vice-Chairman shall be elected for a term of one year. They shall be eligible for re-election.

Rule 17
Acting Chairman

In the absence of the Chairman, the Vice-Chairman shall take the place of the Chairman. If the Chairman ceases to hold office pursuant to rule 18, the Vice-Chairman shall take his or her place until the election of a new Chairman.

Rule 18
Replacement of the Chairman

If the Chairman ceases to be able to carry out his or her functions or ceases to be a member of the Commission, a new Chairman shall be elected for the remainder of the term.

Rule 19
Functions of the Chairman

1. The Chairman shall preside over the meetings of the Commission as provided for under rule 29 of these Rules.
2. The Chairman, or any other member designated by the Commission, shall represent the Commission in that capacity in the Council and, at the invitation of the Council, shall attend meetings of the Council and respond to questions when a matter of particular relevance or complexity relating to the work of the Commission is under consideration by the Council.
3. Such attendance shall not preclude the holding of concurrent meetings of the Council and the Commission.

Rule 20
Exercise of the Chairman's functions

The Chairman, in the exercise of his or her functions and powers as provided for under rules 19 and 29, remains under the authority of the Commission.

V. SECRETARIAT

Rule 21
Duties of the Secretary-General

1.   The Secretary-General shall act in that capacity in all meetings of the Commission. The Secretary-General may designate a member of the Secretariat to act as his or her representative. The Secretary-General shall perform such other administrative functions as are requested of him or her by the Commission.

2.   The Secretary-General shall provide and direct the staff required by the Commission, taking into account to the greatest extent possible the requirements of economy and efficiency, and be responsible for all the arrangements that may be necessary for its meetings.

3.   The Secretary-General shall keep the members of the Commission informed of any matter which is dealt with by other organs of the Authority and which may be of interest to the Commission.

4.   The Secretary-General shall provide to the Commission, at its request, reports on questions specified by the Commission.

Rule 22
Duties of the Secretariat

The Secretariat shall receive, translate, reproduce and distribute recommendations, reports and other documents of the Commission; interpret speeches made at the meeting; prepare and circulate, if so decided by the Commission in accordance with rule 23, the records of the session; have custody and proper preservation of the documents in the archives of the Commission; and, generally, perform all other administrative functions which the Commission may require.

Rule 23
Records and sound recordings of meetings

1.   The Commission may decide to keep summary records of its meetings; but all decisions taken by the Commission shall be duly included in the published records of the Commission. As a general rule they shall be circulated as soon as possible to all members of the Commission, who shall inform the Secretariat within five working days after the circulation of the summary record of any changes they wish to have made.

2.   The Secretariat shall make and retain sound recordings of the meetings of the Commission when it so decides.

VI. LANGUAGES

Rule 24
Languages of the Commission

Arabic, Chinese, English, French, Russian and Spanish shall be the languages of the Commission.

Rule 25
Interpretation

Speeches made in any of the six languages of the Commission shall be interpreted into the other five languages.

Rule 26
Interpretation from a language other than the languages of the Commission

Any member may make a speech in a language other than the languages of the Commission. In this case, he or she shall himself or herself provide for interpretation into one of the languages of the Commission. Interpretation into the other languages of the Commission by the interpreters of the Secretariat may be based on the interpretation given in the first such language.

Rule 27
Languages of recommendations and reports

All recommendations and reports of the Commission shall be published in the languages of the Commission.

VII. CONDUCT OF BUSINESS

Rule 28
Quorum

A majority of the members of the Commission shall constitute a quorum.

Rule 29
Powers of the Chairman

In addition to exercising the powers conferred upon him or her elsewhere in these Rules, the Chairman shall declare the opening and closing of each meeting of the Commission, direct the discussions, ensure observance of these Rules, accord the right to speak, put questions to the vote and announce decisions. The Chairman shall rule on points of order and, subject to these Rules, shall have complete control of the proceedings of the Commission and over the maintenance of order at its meetings. The Chairman may, in the course of the discussion of an item, propose to the Commission the limitation of time to be allowed to speakers, the limitation of the number of times each member may speak on any question, the closure of the list of speakers or the closure of the debate. The Chairman may also propose the suspension or the adjournment of the meeting or of the debate on the question under discussion.

Rule 30

Speeches

The Chairman shall call upon speakers in the order in which they signify their desire to speak. The Chairman may call a speaker to order if his or her remarks are not relevant to the subject under discussion.

Rule 31

Statements by the Secretariat

The Secretary-General, or a member of the Secretariat designated by the Secretary-General as his or her representative, may at any time make either oral or written statements to the Commission concerning any questions under consideration by it.

Rule 32

Points of order

During the discussion of any matter, a member may rise to a point of order, and the point of order shall be immediately decided by the Chairman in accordance with the rules of procedure. A member may appeal against the ruling of the Chairman. The appeal shall be immediately put to the vote, and the Chairman's ruling shall stand unless overruled by a majority of the members present and voting. A member rising to a point of order may not speak on the substance of the matter under discussion.

Rule 33

Time limit on speeches

The Commission may limit the time to be allowed to each speaker and the number of times each member may speak on any question. Before a decision is taken, two members may speak in favour of, and two against, a proposal to set such limits. When the debate is limited and a member exceeds his or her allocated time, the Chairman shall call him or her to order without delay.

Rule 34

Closing of list of speakers

During the course of a debate, the Chairman may announce the list of speakers and, with the consent of the Commission, declare the list closed. The Chairman may, however, accord the right of reply to any member if a speech delivered after he or she has declared the list closed makes this desirable.

Rule 35

Adjournment of debate

During the discussion of any matter, a member may move the adjournment of the debate on the item under discussion. In addition to the proposer of the motion, two members may speak in favour of, and two against, the motion, after which the motion shall be immediately put to the vote. The Chairman may limit the time to be allowed to speakers under this rule.

Rule 36
Closure of debate

A member may at any time move the closure of the debate on the question under discussion, whether or not any other member has signified his wish to speak. Permission to speak on the motion shall be accorded only to two members opposing the closure, after which the motion shall be immediately put to the vote. If the Commission is in favour of the closure, the Chairman shall declare the closure of the debate. The Chairman may limit the time to be allowed to members under this rule.

Rule 37
Suspension or adjournment of the meeting

During the discussion of any matter, a member may move the suspension or the adjournment of the meeting. Such motions shall not be debated, but shall be immediately put to the vote. The Chairman may limit the time to be allowed to the speaker moving the suspension or adjournment of the meeting.

Rule 38
Order of procedural motions

Subject to rule 32, the following motions shall have precedence in the following order over all other proposals or motions before the meeting:
  (a) To suspend the meeting;
  (b) To adjourn the meeting;
  (c) To adjourn the debate on the item under discussion;
  (d) To close the debate on the item under discussion.

Rule 39
Proposals and amendments

Proposals and amendments shall normally be submitted in writing to the Secretary-General, who shall circulate copies to the members of the Commission. As a general rule, no proposal shall be discussed or put to the vote at any meeting of the Commission unless copies of it have been circulated to all members not later than twenty-four hours before the meeting. The Chairman may, however, permit the discussion and consideration of amendments, or of motions as to procedure, even though such amendments and motions have not been circulated or have only been circulated the same day.

Rule 40
Decision on competence

Subject to rule 38, any motion calling for a decision on the competence of the Commission to adopt a proposal submitted to it shall be put to the vote before a decision is taken on the proposal in question.

Rule 41
Withdrawal of proposals and motions

A proposal or a motion may be withdrawn by its proposer at any time before voting on it has commenced, provided that it has not been amended. A proposal or a motion thus withdrawn may be reintroduced by any member.

Rule 42
Reconsideration of proposals

When a proposal has been adopted or rejected, it may not be reconsidered at the same meeting unless the Commission, by a majority of the members present and voting, so decides. Permission to speak on a motion to reconsider shall be accorded only to two speakers opposing the motion, after which it shall be immediately put to the vote.

VIII. DECISION-MAKING

Rule 43
Voting rights

Each member of the Commission shall have one vote.

Rule 44
Decision-making by consensus and voting

1.   As a general rule, decision-making in the Commission should be by consensus.
2.   If all efforts to reach a decision by consensus have been exhausted, decisions by voting shall be taken by a majority of members present and voting.
3.   For the purpose of this rule, "consensus" means the absence of any formal objection.

Rule 45
Meaning of the phrase "members present and voting"

For the purposes of these Rules, the phrase "members present and voting" means members present at the meeting and casting an affirmative or negative vote. Members who abstain from voting shall be considered as not voting.

Rule 46
Recommendations to the Council

Recommendations to the Council shall, wherever necessary, be accompanied by a summary on the divergences of opinion in the Commission.

Rule 47
Method of voting

1.   The Commission shall, in the absence of mechanical means for voting, vote by show of hands, but any member may request a roll-call. The roll-call shall be taken

in the English alphabetical order of the names of the members participating in that session, beginning with the member whose name is drawn by lot by the Chairman. The name of each member shall be called in any roll- call, and the member shall reply "yes" or "no" or "abstention". The result of the voting shall be inserted in the record in the English alphabetical order of the names of the members.

2.   When the Commission votes by mechanical means, a non-recorded vote shall replace a vote by show of hands and a recorded vote shall replace a roll-call vote. Any member may request a recorded vote. In the case of a recorded vote, the Commission shall, unless a member requests otherwise, dispense with the procedure of calling out the names of the members; nevertheless, the result of the voting shall be inserted in the record in the same manner as that of a roll-call vote.

Rule 48
Conduct during voting

After the Chairman has announced the beginning of voting, no member shall interrupt the voting, except on a point of order in connection with the actual process of the voting.

Rule 49
Explanation of vote

Members may make brief statements consisting solely of explanations of their votes before the voting has commenced or after the voting has been completed. The member sponsoring a proposal or motion shall not speak in explanation of vote thereon, except if it has been amended.

Rule 50
Division of proposals and amendments

A member may move that parts of a proposal or of an amendment should be voted upon separately. If objection is made to the request for division, the motion for division shall be voted upon. Permission to speak on the motion for division shall be given only to two speakers in favour and two speakers against. If the motion for division is carried, those parts of the proposal or of the amendments which are approved shall then be put to the vote as a whole. If all operative parts of the proposal or of the amendments have been rejected, the proposal or the amendments shall be considered to have been rejected as a whole.

Rule 51
Order of voting on amendments

When an amendment is moved to a proposal, the amendment shall be voted upon first. When two or more amendments are moved to a proposal, the Commission shall first vote on the amendment furthest removed in substance from the original proposal and then on the amendment next furthest removed therefrom, and so on until all the amendments have been put to the vote. Where, however, the adoption of one amendment necessarily implies the rejection of another amendment, the latter amendment shall not be put to the vote. If one or more amendments are adopted, the amended proposal shall then be voted upon. A motion is considered an amendment to a proposal if it merely adds to, deletes from or revises part of the proposal.

Rule 52
Order of voting on proposals

If two or more proposals relate to the same question, the Commission shall, unless it decides otherwise, vote on the proposals in the order in which they have been submitted. The Commission may, after each vote on a proposal, decide whether to vote on the next proposal.

IX. PARTICIPATION BY NON-MEMBERS OF THE COMMISSION

Rule 53
Participation by members of the Authority and entities carrying out activities in the Area

1.   Any member of the Authority may, with the permission of the Commission, send a representative to attend a meeting of the Commission when a matter particularly affecting such member is under consideration. For the purpose of facilitating the work of the Commission, such representative shall be allowed to express his or her views on any such matter being considered by the Commission.

2.   The Commission may invite any State or entity carrying out activities in the Area for the purposes of consultation and collaboration, where the Commission considers appropriate.

3.   The members of the Commission shall, upon request by any member of the Authority or other party concerned, be accompanied by a representative of such member or other party concerned when carrying out their function of supervision and inspection.

4.   Any member of the Authority may make a request to the Secretary-General to convene a meeting of the Commission in order to consider a matter of particular concern to that member involving an environmental emergency. The Secretary-General shall convene the Commission which shall give urgent consideration to such matter and report to the Council as soon as possible with its findings and recommendations. Any member concerned with such matter has the right to send a representative to the meeting of the Commission to express its views on the matter without participation in decision-making, although the Commission may determine that such presence be limited at certain stages when confidential information is being discussed.

Rule 54
Entry into force

These Rules of Procedure shall enter into force on the date of their approval by the Council.

COMMENTARY

The Preparatory Commission had prepared draft rules of procedure for the Legal and Technical Commission (LOS/PCN/WP.31/Rev.3). However, as with the rules of procedure of other organs of the Authority, these needed to be modified in order to bring them into conformity with the provisions of the Agreement.

Following the election of the first Legal and Technical Commission in 1996, the Commission considered a revised draft rules of procedure prepared by the Secretariat (ISBA/3/LTC/WP.3). It completed work on the draft during the resumed fourth session of the Authority (August 1998) and, on 26 August 1998, adopted an informal revised text which was submitted to the Council at the fifth session of the Authority for approval in accordance with article 163, paragraph 10, of the Convention.

During the fifth session (1999), the Council considered the draft rules of procedure of the Legal and Technical Commission proposed by the Commission (ISBA/5/C/L.1). Following detailed examination of the draft, the Secretariat prepared a revised text for further consideration by the Council (ISBA/5/C/L.1/Rev.1). After further consideration of the draft, at its fifty-eighth meeting, on 26 August 1999, the Council approved the rules of procedure as contained in document ISBA/5/C/L.1/Rev.2, with the exception of rules 6 (meetings) and 53 (participation by members of the Authority and entities carrying out activities in the Area), which were to be considered further at the sixth session of the Authority.

At the sixth session (2000), following discussion of the pending rules, a revised text of the rules of procedure was produced (ISBA/6/C/L.4). At its sixty-eighth meeting, on 13 July 2000, the Council approved the rules of procedure of the Legal and Technical Commission, as contained in document ISBA/6/C/9.

DOCUMENTARY SOURCES

- PREPARATORY COMMISSION
LOS/PCN/WP.31/Rev.3, Final draft rules of procedure of the Legal and Technical Commission, reproduced in: LOS/PCN/153, Vol. V, p. 58-74.
- ISBA
ISBA/4/A/11, Report of the Secretary-General of the International Seabed Authority under article 166, paragraph 4, of the United Nations Convention on the Law of the Sea, para. 57, (*Selected Decisions 4*, 62).
ISBA/5/A/1 and Corr. 1, Report of the Secretary-General of the International Seabed Authority under article 166, paragraph 4, of the United Nations Convention on the Law of the Sea, para. 52, (*Selected Decisions 5*, 11).

ISBA/6/A/9, Report of the Secretary-General of the International Seabed Authority under article 166, paragraph 4, of the United Nations Convention on the Law of the Sea, para. 5, (*Selected Decisions 6*, 13).

ISBA/4/C/14, Statement of the President on the work of the Council during the resumed fourth session, para. 7, (*Selected Decisions 4*, 76).

ISBA/5/C/L.1, Draft rules of procedure of the Legal and Technical Commission. Proposed by the Legal and Technical Commission.

ISBA/5/C/L.1/Rev.1, Draft rules of procedure of the Legal and Technical Commission. Proposed by the Legal and Technical Commission.

ISBA/5/C/L.1/Rev.2, Draft rules of procedure of the Legal and Technical Commission. Proposed by the Legal and Technical Commission.

ISBA/5/C/11, Statement of the President on the work of the Council at the fifth session, para. 15, (*Selected Decisions 5*, 49).

ISBA/6/C/3, Statement of the President on the work of the Council at the sixth session, paras. 7 and 9, (*Selected Decisions 6*, 71).

ISBA/6/C/9, Decision of the Council of the Authority concerning the rules of procedure of the Legal and Technical Commission, (*Selected Decisions 6*, 73-83).

ISBA/6/C/13, Statement of the President on the work of the Council at the resumed sixth session, para. 4, (*Selected Decisions 6*, 87).

ISBA/6/C/L.4, Draft decision of the Council of the Authority concerning the rules of procedure of the Legal and Technical Commission.

ISBA/3/LTC/WP.3, Draft rules of procedure of the Legal and Technical Commission.

DECISION OF THE COUNCIL OF THE INTERNATIONAL SEABED AUTHORITY ON THE FUTURE SIZE AND COMPOSITION OF THE LEGAL AND TECHNICAL COMMISSION AND THE PROCESS FOR FUTURE ELECTIONS[1]

The Council of the International Seabed Authority,

Recalling the provisions of article 163 of the United Nations Convention on the Law of the Sea, including the requirement that the Legal and Technical Commission shall be composed of 15 members, elected by the Council from among the candidates nominated by the States parties; the Council may decide, if necessary, to increase the size of the Commission giving due regard to economy and efficiency,

Recalling also the provisions of article 165, paragraph 1, of the Convention, which provides that members of the Legal and Technical Commission shall have appropriate qualifications such as those relevant to exploration for and exploitation and processing of mineral resources, oceanology, protection of the marine environment, or economic or legal matters relating to ocean mining and related fields of expertise,

1. *Decides* that the procedure for nomination of candidates for future elections of the Legal and Technical Commission shall be as follows:

(a) At least six months before the opening of the session of the International Seabed Authority at which the election is to be held, the Secretary-General shall address a written invitation to all members of the Authority to submit their nominations of candidates for election to the Commission;

(b) Nominations for election to the Commission shall be accompanied by a statement of qualification or curriculum vitae setting out the candidate's qualifications and expertise in fields relevant to the work of the Commission and shall be received not less than three months prior to the opening of the relevant session of the Authority; nominations received less than three months prior to the opening of the relevant session of the Authority will not be accepted;

(c)　The Secretary-General shall prepare a list in alphabetical order of the persons nominated for election to the Commission in accordance with paragraph (a) above, indicating the nominating member of the Authority, and containing an annex with the statements of qualification or curricula vitae submitted in accordance with paragraph (b) above; the list shall be circulated to all members of the Authority not less than two months prior to the opening of the session at which the election is to be held;

2.　*Requests* the Secretary-General, taking into account the views of the chairs of the Legal and Technical Commission, to prepare a report for consideration by the Council in 2010 on the functioning of the Commission, with a view to the Council determining in 2010 the number of members of the Commission to be elected in 2011.

COMMENTARY

For the regular elections of members of the Commission in 1996, 2001 and 2006, the procedure was that the Council approved all the candidacies that had been submitted. However late submissions made evaluation of candidates by the Council difficult. At the second election of the Commission in 2001, the Council requested that nominations should be submitted to the Secretary-General within two months of the opening of the session at which the election would take place, in order to allow sufficient time for the Council to review the nominations. The same process was followed for the election in 2006. In spite of the Council's request, many nominations were received less than two months before the election. However, in the absence of a firm decision by the Council on a closing date for submissions, the Secretary-General considered that he had no discretion to reject late submissions. Following the election in 2006, the Council requested the Secretary-General to prepare a note on the future size and composition of the Legal and Technical Commission and the process for future elections for its consideration in 2007.

During the thirteenth session of the Authority in 2007, the Council took note of the report in question, which recommended that the Council consider adopting clear guidelines for the conduct of elections, modelled on the relevant provisions regarding the process for elections of judges as set out in the Statute of the International Tribunal for the Law of the Sea. On 18 July 2007, the Council agreed that there was a need to streamline the procedure for future elections in order to avoid some of the difficulties that had arisen in past elections. The Council agreed on a procedure for the nomination of candidates for future elections and its decision is contained in document ISBA/13/C/6. At least six months before the opening of the session at which there is an election to the Commission, the Secretary-General invites in writing members of the Authority to submit nominations along with curricula vitate of the candidates within three months, indicating that late nominations will not be accepted. The list of the nominations and the curricula vitae is then circulated to members of the Authority no later than two months before the session where the election is to be held.

At its one hundred and fifty-second and one hundred and fifty-third meetings, on 29 and 30 April 2010, the Council recalled its decision ISBA/13/C/6 and agreed that the streamlined procedures must be applied strictly.

The Council had the first opportunity to apply its decision ISBA/13/C/6 during the seventeenth session held in 2011 with the election of the membership of the Commission for the period 2012 to 2016. Members of the Council regretted that some nominations had not been submitted in time. Nevertheless, the Council noted that the total number of candidates for election did not exceed 25, as agreed in 2010. However, for future elections, members of the Council emphasized the importance of strictly following the agreed procedures as set out in the decision ISBA/13/C/6.

DOCUMENTARY SOURCES

- ISBA

ISBA/7/C/7, Statement of the President on the work of the Council at the seventh session, para. 6, (*Selected Decisions 7*, 37).

ISBA/11/C/11, Statement of the President on the work of the Council at the eleventh session, para. 11, (*Selected Decisions 11*, 44).

ISBA/12/C/11, Decision of the Council relating to the election of members of the Legal and Technical Commission, (*Selected Decisions 12*, 39-40).

ISBA/13/A/7, Statement of the President on the work of the Assembly at the thirteenth session, para. 11, (*Selected Decisions 13*, 30).

ISBA/13/C/2, Considerations relating to the future size and composition of the Legal and Technical Commission and the process for future elections.

ISBA/13/C/6, Decision of the Council of the International Seabed Authority on the future size and composition of the Legal and Technical Commission and the process for future elections, (*Selected Decisions 13*, 41-42).

ISBA/13/C/7, Statement of the President on the work of the Council at the thirteenth session, paras. 7-8, (*Selected Decisions 13*, 43).

ISBA/16/C/3, Considerations relating to the functioning of the Legal and Technical Commission, (*Selected Decisions 16*, 81-85).

ISBA/16/C/7, Summary Report of the Chairman of the Legal and Technical Commission on the work of the Commission during the sixteenth session, paras. 25-26, (*Selected Decisions 16*, 105).

ISBA/16/C/14*, Statement of the President of the Council of the International Seabed Authority on the work of the Council during the sixteenth session, paras. 11-13, (*Selected Decisions 16*, 111).

ISBA/17/C/21*, Statement of the President of the Council of the International Seabed Authority on the work of the Council during the seventeenth session, paras. 17-19, (*Selected Decisions 17*, 117).

B – FINANCIAL REGULATIONS OF THE INTERNATIONAL SEABED AUTHORITY

Table Of Contents

INTRODUCTORY NOTE

The United Nations Convention on the Law of the Sea entered into force on 16 November 1994. On 28 July 1994, the General Assembly of the United Nations adopted the Agreement relating to the Implementation of Part XI of the United Nations Convention on the Law of the Sea of 10 December 1982. The Agreement has been provisionally applied since 16 November 1994 and entered into force on 28 July 1996.

According to the Agreement, its provisions and Part XI of the Convention shall be interpreted and applied together as a single instrument; these Regulations and references in these Regulations to the Convention shall be interpreted and applied accordingly.

Adjustments and additions to these Regulations will be needed when the Authority has sufficient income to meet its administrative expenses from sources other than assessed contributions of the members of the Authority.

Regulation 1
Applicability

1.1 These Regulations shall govern the financial administration of the International Seabed Authority.

1.2 For the purpose of these Regulations:

(a) "Agreement" means the Agreement relating to the Implementation of Part XI of the United Nations Convention on the Law of the Sea of 10 December 1982;

(b) "Authority" means the International Seabed Authority;

(c) "Convention" means the United Nations Convention on the Law of the Sea of 10 December 1982;

(d) "member of the Authority" means:

    (i) any State Party to the Convention; and

    (ii) any provisional member;

(e) "Secretary-General" means the Secretary-General of the International Seabed Authority.

Regulation 2
The financial period

2.1 The financial period shall consist of two consecutive calendar years.

Regulation 3
The budget

3.1 The proposed budget for each financial period shall be prepared by the Secretary-General.

3.2 The proposed budget shall cover income and expenditures for the financial period to which they relate and shall be presented in United States dollars.

3.3 The proposed budget shall be divided into parts and sections and, when appropriate, programmes. The proposed budget shall be accompanied by such information annexes and explanatory statements as may be necessary for the consideration of the budget, including a statement on the main changes in the content in comparison with the previous financial period, as well as its programmatic contents where applicable, and such further annexes or statements as the Secretary-General may deem necessary and useful.

3.4 The Secretary-General shall, in the second year of a financial period, submit his proposed budget for the following financial period to the Council, which shall submit it to the Assembly, together with its recommendations thereon. The Secretary-General shall transmit his proposed budget to the members of the Finance Committee at least forty-five days prior to the meeting of the Finance Committee at which the proposed budget is to be considered. The proposed budget shall be transmitted to all members of the Authority at least forty-five days prior to the opening of the session of the Council and the Assembly.

3.5 The Finance Committee shall prepare a report for the consideration of the Council on the budget proposed by the Secretary-General, containing the recommendations of the Finance Committee.

3.6 The Council shall consider the report of the Finance Committee and submit the proposed budget to the Assembly, with any recommendations. The Assembly shall consider and approve the budget for the following financial period submitted by the Council, on the understanding that the budget for the financial period will be appropriated annually in accordance with the Convention.

3.7 Decisions by the Assembly and the Council on the administrative budget of the Authority shall take into account the recommendations of the Finance Committee.

3.8 Supplementary budget proposals may be submitted by the Secretary-General if exceptional circumstances make this necessary.

3.9 Supplementary budget proposals shall be prepared in a form consistent with the approved budget. The provisions of these Regulations shall be applicable to the proposed supplementary budget to the extent possible. Decisions of the Council and the Assembly on the supplementary budget proposed by the Secretary-General shall take into account the recommendations of the Finance Committee.

3.10 The Secretary-General may enter into commitments for future financial periods, provided that such commitments do not affect the current budget and:

(a) are for activities which leave been approved by the Council or the Assembly and are expected to continue beyond the end of the current financial period; or

(b) are authorized by specific decisions of the Council or the Assembly.

Regulation 4
Appropriations

4.1 The appropriations voted by the Assembly shall constitute an authorization to the Secretary-General to incur obligations and make payments for the purposes for which the appropriations were voted and up to the amounts so voted.

4.2 Appropriations shall be available for obligations during the financial period to which they relate.

4.3 Appropriations shall remain available for twelve months following the end of the financial period to which they relate to the extent that they are required to discharge obligations in respect of goods supplied and services rendered in the financial period and to liquidate any other outstanding legal obligation of the financial period. The balance of the appropriations shall be surrendered.

4.4 At the end of the twelve-month period provided in regulation 4.3 above, the then remaining balance of any appropriations retained will be surrendered. Any unliquidated obligations of the financial period in question shall, at that time, be cancelled or, where the obligation remains a valid charge, transferred as an obligation against current appropriations.

4.5 Transfers between appropriation sections may only be made to the extent authorized by the Assembly.

4.6 The Secretary-General shall prudently manage the appropriations voted for a financial period, taking into account the availability of cash balances.

Regulation 5
Funds

5.1 There shall be established a general administrative fund for the purpose of accounting for the administrative expenditures of the Authority. The contributions paid under regulation 6.1 (a) and (b) by members of the Authority, income from the Enterprise, miscellaneous income and any advances made from the working capital fund to finance administrative expenditure shall be credited to the general administrative fund.

5.2   There shall be established a working capital fund in an amount and for purposes to be determined from time to time by the Assembly. The source of moneys of the working capital fund shall be advances from members of the Authority until the Authority shall have sufficient income from other sources to meet its administrative expenses, and these advances, made in accordance with an agreed scale of assessment based upon the scale used for the regular budget of the United Nations or, in the case of international organizations, as determined by the Authority, shall be carried to the credit of members which have made such advances.

5.3   Advances made from the working capital fund to finance budgetary appropriations shall be reimbursed to the fund as soon as income is available for that purpose.

5.4   Income derived from investments of the working capital fund shall be credited to miscellaneous income.

5.5   Trust funds, reserve and special accounts may be established by the Secretary-General and shall be reported to the Finance Committee.

5.6   The purpose and limits of each trust fund, reserve and special account shall be clearly defined by the appropriate organ of the Authority. Unless otherwise provided by the Assembly, such funds and accounts shall be administered in accordance with the present Regulations.

5.7   The administrative expenses of the Authority shall be a first call upon the funds of the Authority. Except for the contributions referred to in regulation 6.1 (a) and (b), the funds which remain after payment of administrative expenses may, *inter alia*:

   (a)   be shared in accordance with article 140 and article 160, paragraph 2 (g), of the Convention;

   (b)   be used to provide the Enterprise with funds in accordance with article 170, paragraph 4, of the Convention; and

   (c)   be set aside for the purposes of the economic assistance fund referred to in paragraph 1 (a) of section 7 of the annex to the Agreement.[1]

5.8   There shall be established an economic assistance fund in accordance with paragraph 1 (a) of section 7 of the annex to the Agreement. The amount set aside for this purpose shall be determined by the Council from time to time, upon the recommendation of the Finance Committee. Only funds from payments received from contractors, including the Enterprise, and voluntary contributions shall be credited to the economic assistance fund, after having covered the administrative expenses of the Authority.[2]

---

[1]   This provision will need to be elaborated in due time.
[2]   This provision will need to be elaborated in due time.

Regulation 6
Provision of funds

6.1 The funds of the Authority shall include:

(a) assessed contributions made by States members of the Authority;

(b) agreed contributions, as determined by the Authority, made by international organizations members of the Authority in accordance with annex IX to the Convention;

(c) funds received by the Authority pursuant to annex III, article 13, paragraph 2, of the Convention and section 8 of the annex to the Agreement, in connection with activities in the Area;

(d) funds transferred from the Enterprise in accordance with annex IV, article 10, of the Convention;

(e) voluntary contributions made by members or other entities; and

(f) such other funds to which the Authority may become entitled or may receive, including income from investment.

6.2 The appropriations, subject to the adjustments effected in accordance with the provisions of regulation 6.3, shall be financed by contributions from the States members of the Authority in accordance with an agreed scale of assessment based upon the scale used for the regular budget of the United Nations, including a floor rate and a ceiling rate as determined from time to time by the Authority, and by contributions from international organizations members of the Authority, as determined from time to time by the Authority, until the Authority shall have sufficient income from other sources to meet its administrative expenses. Pending the receipt of such contributions, the appropriations may be financed from the working capital fund.

6.3 For each of the two years of a financial period, the contributions of the members of the Authority shall be assessed on the basis of half of the appropriations approved by the Assembly for that financial period, except that adjustments shall be made to the assessments in respect of:

(a) supplementary appropriations for which contributions have not previously been assessed on members of the Authority;

(b) half of the estimated miscellaneous income for the financial period for which credits have not previously been taken into account, and any adjustments in estimated miscellaneous income previously taken into account;

(c) contributions resulting from the assessment of new members of the Authority under the provisions of regulation 6.9;

(d) any balance of the appropriations surrendered under regulations 4.3 and 4.4.

6.4 After the Assembly has adopted or revised the budget and determined the amount of the working capital fund, the Secretary-General shall:

(a) transmit the relevant documents to the members of the Authority;

(b) inform the members of the Authority of their contributions in respect of annual contributions and advances to the working capital fund; and

(c) request them to remit their contributions and advances.

6.5   Contributions and advances shall be considered as due and payable in full within thirty days of the receipt of the communication of the Secretary-General referred to in regulation 6.4 above, or as of the first day of the calendar year to which they relate, whichever is the later. As of 1 January of the following calendar year, the unpaid balance of such contributions and advances shall be considered to be one year in arrears.

6.6   Annual contributions and advances to the working capital fund shall be assessed and paid in United States dollars.

6.7   Payments made by a member of the Authority shall be credited first to the working capital fund and then to the contributions due, in the order in which the member was assessed.

6.8   The Secretary-General shall submit to each regular session of the Assembly, the Council and the Finance Committee a report on the collection of contributions and advances to the working capital fund.

6.9   New members shall be required to make a contribution for the year in which they become members of the Authority and to provide their proportion of the total advances to the working capital fund at rates to be determined by the Assembly.

6.10 States and entities referred to in article 305 of the Convention which are not members of the Authority but which participate in its activities shall contribute to the expenses of the Authority at rates to be determined by the Assembly, unless the Assembly decides with respect to any such State or entity to exempt it from the requirement of so contributing. Such contributions shall be taken into account as miscellaneous income.

Regulation 7
Other income

7.1   All other income except:
(a)   contributions to the budget;
(b)   funds received by the Authority pursuant to annex III, article 13, para-
        graph 3, of the Convention and section 8 of the annex to the Agreement,
        in connection with activities in the Area;
(c)   funds transferred from the Enterprise in accordance with annex IV, article
        10, of the Convention;
(d)   voluntary contributions made by members or other entities;
(e)   payments received by the Authority pursuant to article 82 of the Convention;
(f)   payments to the economic assistance fund, in accordance with paragraph
        1 (a) of section 7 of the annex to the Agreement;
(g)   direct refunds of expenditures made during the financial period;
(h)   advances or deposits to funds; and
(i)   revenue derived from the Staff Assessment Plan,
shall be classed as miscellaneous income, for credit to the general administrative fund.

7.2   Voluntary contributions, whether or not in cash, may be accepted by the Secretary-General provided that the purposes for which the contributions are made are consistent with the policies, aims and activities of the Authority, and provided that the acceptance of such contributions which directly or indirectly involve additional financial liability for the Authority shall require the consent of the appropriate authority.

7.3 Moneys accepted for purposes specified by the donor shall be treated as trust funds or special accounts under regulations 5.5 and 5.6.

7.4 Moneys accepted in respect of which no purpose is specified shall be treated as miscellaneous income and reported as "gifts" in the accounts of the financial period.

Regulation 8
Custody of funds

8.1 The Secretary-General shall designate the bank or banks in which the funds of the Authority shall be kept. The Secretary-General shall from time to time report to the Council on the designation of such bank or banks.

Regulation 9
Investment of funds

9.1 The Secretary-General may make short-term investments of a non-speculative nature, of moneys not needed for immediate requirements and shall inform the Finance Committee periodically of such investments which he or she has made.

9.2 The Secretary-General may, after consultations with an investment counsellor appointed on the recommendation of the Finance Committee, make long-term investments of moneys standing to the credit of trust funds, reserve and special accounts, except as may be otherwise provided by the appropriate authority in respect of each such fund or account and having regard to the particular requirements as to the liquidity of funds in each case.

9.3 Income derived from investments shall be credited as provided in the rules relating to each fund or account.

Regulation 10
Internal control

10.1 The Secretary-General shall:
(a) establish detailed financial rules and procedures in order to ensure effective financial administration and the exercise of economy;
(b) cause all payments to be made on the basis of supporting vouchers and other documents which ensure that the services or goods have been received and that payments have not previously been made;
(c) designate the officers who may receive moneys, incur obligations and make payments on behalf of the Authority;
(d) maintain an internal financial control which shall provide for an effective current examination and/or review of financial transactions in order to ensure:
   (i) the regularity of the receipt, custody and disposal of all funds and other financial resources of the Authority;
   (ii) the conformity of obligations and expenditures with the appropriations or other financial provisions voted by the Assembly, or with the purposes and rules relating to trust funds and special accounts;

(iii) the economic use of the resources of the Authority.

10.2 Obligations for the current financial period or commitments for current and future financial periods shall be incurred only after allotments or other appropriations have been made in writing under the authority of the Secretary-General.

10.3 The Secretary-General may make such ex gratia payments as he or she deems to be necessary in the interest of the Authority, provided that a statement of such payments shall be submitted to the Assembly with the accounts.

10.4 The Secretary-General may, after full investigation, authorize the writing-off of losses of cash, stores and other assets, provided that a statement of all such amounts written off shall be submitted to the Auditor with the accounts together with the justifications attached thereto.

10.5 Tenders for equipment, supplies and other requirements shall be invited by advertisement, except where the Secretary-General deems that, in the interests of the Authority, a departure from the rules is desirable.

Regulation 11
The accounts

11.1 The Secretary-General shall submit accounts for the financial period. In addition, the Secretary-General shall maintain, for management purposes, such accounting records as are necessary, including interim accounts for the first calendar year of the financial period. Both the interim accounts and the accounts for the financial period shall show:
  (a) the income and expenditures of all funds;
  (b) the status of appropriations, including:
      (i) the original budget appropriations;
      (ii) the appropriations as modified by any transfers;
      (iii) credits, if any, other than the appropriations voted by the Assembly;
      (iv) the amounts charged against those appropriations and/or other credits;
  (c) the assets and liabilities of the Authority.
The Secretary-General shall also give such other information as may be appropriate to indicate the current financial position of the Authority.

11.2 The accounts of the Authority shall be presented in United States dollars. Accounting records may, however, be kept in such currency or currencies as the Secretary-General may deem necessary.

11.3 Appropriate separate accounts shall be maintained for all trust funds, reserve and special accounts.

11.4 The accounts for the financial period shall be submitted by the Secretary-General to the Auditor not later than 31 March following the end of the financial period.

Regulation 12
Audit

12.1 The Assembly shall appoint an internationally recognized independent auditor with experience in the audit of international organizations. The independent auditor shall be appointed for a period of four years and may be reappointed for one term.

12.2 The audit shall be conducted in conformity with generally accepted common auditing standards and, subject to any special directions of the Assembly, in accordance with the additional terms of reference set out in the annex to the present Regulations.

12.3 The Auditor shall, as appropriate, make observations with respect to the efficiency of the financial procedures, the accounting system, the internal financial controls and, in general, the administration and management of the Authority.

12.4 The Auditor shall be completely independent and solely responsible for the conduct of the audit.

12.5 The Finance Committee may request the Auditor to perform certain specific examinations and issue separate reports on the results.

12.6 The Secretary-General shall provide the Auditor with the facilities he or she may require in the performance of the audit.

12.7 The Auditor shall issue a report on the audit of the financial statements and relevant schedules relating to the accounts for the financial period, which shall include such information as the Auditor deems necessary with regard to matters referred to in regulation 12.3 and in the additional terms of reference.

12.8 The Finance Committee shall examine the financial statements and the audit reports and shall forward them to the Council and the Assembly, with such comments as it deems appropriate.

Regulation 13
Resolutions involving expenditures

13.1 Decisions by the Assembly or the Council having financial or budgetary implications shall be based on the recommendations of the Finance Committee.

13.2 No organ or subsidiary body of the Authority shall take a decision involving either a change in the budget approved by the Assembly or the possible requirement of expenditure unless it has received and taken account of a report by the Secretary-General on the budget implications of the proposal, and any recommendations of the Finance Committee.

13.3 Where, in the opinion of the Secretary-General, the proposed expenditure cannot be made from existing appropriations, it shall not be incurred until the Assembly has made the necessary appropriations.

Regulation 14
General provisions

14.1 These Regulations shall become effective on the date they are approved by the Assembly and shall apply to the financial period 2001-2002 and to subsequent financial periods. They may be amended only by the Assembly.

ANNEX

ADDITIONAL TERMS OF REFERENCE GOVERNING THE AUDIT OF THE AUTHORITY

1.   The Auditors shall perform the audits of the accounts of the Authority, including all trust funds and special accounts, as they deem necessary in order to satisfy themselves:

    (a) that the financial statements are in accord with the books and records of the Authority;

    (b) that the financial transactions reflected in the statements have been in accordance with the financial rules and regulations, the budgetary provisions and other applicable directives;

    (c) that the securities and moneys on deposit and on hand have been verified by certificates received directly from the Authority's depositaries or by actual count;

    (d) that the internal controls, including internal oversight, are adequate in the light of the extent of reliance placed thereupon.

2.   The Auditors shall be the sole judge as to the acceptance in whole or in part of certifications and representations by the Secretary-General and may proceed to such detailed examination and verification as they choose of all financial records, including those relating to supplies and equipment.

3.   The Auditors and their staff shall have free access at all convenient times to all books, records and other documents which are, in the opinion of the Auditors, necessary for the performance of the audit. The Auditors shall be responsible for the work done by such supporting staff in the conduct of auditing. Information which is classified as privileged and which the Secretary-General (or the Secretary-General's designated senior official) agrees is required by the Auditors for the purposes of the audit and information classified as confidential shall be made available on application. The Auditors and their staff shall respect the privileged and confidential nature of any information so classified which has been made available and shall not make use of it except in direct connection with the performance of the audit. The Auditors may draw the attention of the Assembly to any denial of information classified as privileged which, in their opinion, was required for the purpose of the audit.

4.   The Auditors shall have no power to disallow items in the accounts but shall draw to the attention of the Secretary-General for appropriate action any transaction concerning which they entertain doubt as to legality or propriety. Audit objections, to these or any other transactions, arising during the examination of the accounts shall be communicated immediately to the Secretary-General.

5.   The Auditors (or such of their officers as they may designate) shall express and sign an opinion on the financial statements which shall read as follows:

    "We have examined the following appended financial statements, numbered .... to .... , properly identified, and relevant schedules of (name of the body) for the financial period ended 31 December 19 __ . Our examination included a general review of the accounting procedures and such tests of the accounting records and other supporting evidence as we considered necessary in the circumstances.",

And which shall state, as appropriate, whether:

(a) the financial statements present fairly the financial position as at the end of the period and the results of its operations for the period then ended;

(b) the financial statements were prepared in accordance with the stated accounting principles;

(c) the accounting principles were applied on a basis consistent with that of the preceding financial period;

(d) transactions were in accordance with the financial regulations and legislative authority.

6.   The report of the Auditors to the Assembly on the financial operations of the period should mention:

(a) the type and scope of their examination;

(b) matters affecting the completeness or accuracy of the accounts, including, where appropriate:

(i) information necessary to the correct interpretation of the accounts;

(ii) any amounts which ought to have been received but which have not been brought to account;

(iii) any amounts for which a legal or contingent obligation exists and which have not been recorded or reflected in the financial statements;

(iv) expenditures not properly substantiated;

(v) whether proper books of accounts have been kept - where in the presentation of statements there are deviations of a material nature from the generally accepted accounting principles applied on a consistent basis, these should be disclosed;

(c) other matters which should be brought to the notice of the Assembly, such as:

(i) cases of fraud;

(ii) wasteful or improper expenditure of the Authority's money or other assets (notwithstanding that the accounting for the transaction may be correct);

(iii) expenditure likely to commit the Authority to further outlay on a large scale;

(iv) any defect in the general system or detailed regulations governing the control of receipts and disbursements or of supplies and equipment;

(v) expenditure not in accordance with the intention of the Assembly after making allowance for duly authorized transfers within the budget;

(vi) expenditure in excess of appropriations as amended by duly authorized transfers within the budget;

(vii) expenditure not in conformity with the authority which governs it;
(d) the accuracy or otherwise of the supplies and equipment records as determined by stock-taking and examination of the records;
(e) if appropriate, transactions accounted for in a previous period concerning which further information has been obtained or transactions in a later period concerning which it seems desirable that the Assembly should have early knowledge.

7.   The Auditors may make such observations with respect to their findings resulting from the audit and such comments on the Secretary-General's financial report as they deem appropriate to the Assembly or to the Secretary-General.

8.   Whenever the scope of the audit of the Auditors is restricted, or whenever they are unable to obtain sufficient evidence, the Auditors shall refer to the matter in their opinion and report, making clear in the report the reasons for their comments and the effect on the financial position and the financial transactions as recorded.

9.   In no case shall the Auditors include criticism in their report without first affording the Secretary-General an adequate opportunity of explanation on the matter under observation.

10.   The Auditors are not required to mention any matter referred to in the foregoing that, in their opinion, is insignificant in all respects.

COMMENTARY

Pending the adoption of its own regulations consistent with the financial regulations of the United Nations, the Authority applied, *mutatis mutandis*, the Financial Regulations of the United Nations. Draft financial regulations were considered and revised by the Finance Committee during the resumed third session of the Authority in August 1997 and again during the first part of the fourth session in March 1998. The Finance Committee completed its work on the draft financial regulations of the Authority at the resumed fourth session of the Authority in August 1998.

At its fortieth meeting, on 27 August 1998, the Council took up consideration of the draft financial regulations proposed by the Finance Committee (ISBA/4/C/L.3). For lack of time, consideration of the draft financial regulations was deferred to the fifth session of the Council in August 1999.

Following a detailed examination of the draft regulations by the Council at the fifth session, the Secretariat prepared a revised text for further consideration by the Council (ISBA/5/C/L.3). At its fifty-seventh meeting, on 26 August 1999, upon the recommendation of the Finance Committee, the Council decided to adopt and apply provisionally the draft financial regulations, pending their approval by the Assembly (ISBA/5/C/10).

The Assembly did not have sufficient time to consider the draft financial regulations of the Authority at the fifth session, although it was noted that the regulations had been adopted by the Council and would apply provisionally. Acting on the recommendation of the Council, the Assembly approved the Financial Regulations of the Authority at its seventy-first meeting, on 23 March 2000 (ISBA/6/A/3).

Pursuant to Regulation 10 of the Financial Regulations, the Secretary-General has established the Financial Rules of the International Seabed Authority, which apply as from 1 December 2008, unless otherwise indicated. The Secretary-General promulgated them on 10 November 2008 (ST/SGB/2008/02) and informed the Finance Committee which took note of them during the sixteenth session of the Authority in 2010.

DOCUMENTARY SOURCES

- ISBA

ISBA/A/15, Decision of the Assembly relating to participation of the International Seabed Authority in the United Nations Joint Staff Pension Fund, (*Selected Decisions 1/2/3*, 29).

ISBA/3/A/4, Report of the Secretary-General of the International Seabed Authority under article 166, paragraph 4, of the United Nations Convention on the Law of the Sea, para. 39, (*Selected Decisions 1/2/3*, 54).

ISBA/3/A/11, Statement of the President on the work of the Assembly during the resumed third session, para. 12, (*Selected Decisions 1/2/3*, 63).

ISBA/4/A/11, Report of the Secretary-General of the International Seabed Authority under article 166, paragraph 4, of the United Nations Convention on the Law of the Sea, paras. 38 and 57, (*Selected Decisions 4*, 58 and 62).

ISBA/4/A/18, Statement of the President on the work of the Assembly during the resumed fourth session, para. 15, (*Selected Decisions 4*, 66).

ISBA/5/A/1 and Corr. 1, Report of the Secretary-General of the International Seabed Authority under article 166, paragraph 4, of the United Nations Convention on the Law of the Sea, paras. 25 and 52, (*Selected Decisions 5*, 5 and 11).

ISBA/5/A/14, Statement of the President on the work of the Assembly at the fifth session, para. 23, (*Selected Decisions 5*, 42).

ISBA/6/A/3, Decision of the Assembly of the International Seabed Authority concerning the Financial Regulations of the International Seabed Authority, (*Selected Decisions 6*, 1-11).

ISBA/6/A/6, Statement of the President on the work of the Assembly at the first part of the sixth session, para. 8, (*Selected Decisions 6*, 12).

ISBA/6/A/9, Report of the Secretary-General of the International Seabed Authority under article 166, paragraph 4, of the United Nations Convention on the Law of the Sea, paras. 5 and 22, (*Selected Decisions 6*, 13 and 16).

ISBA/6/A/L.2, Draft decision of the Assembly of the International Seabed Authority concerning the Financial Regulations of the International Seabed Authority.

ISBA/3/C/11, Statement of the President on the work of the Council during the resumed third session, para. 1, (*Selected Decisions 1/2/3*, 72).

ISBA/4/C/5, Statement of the President on the work of the Council during the first part of the fourth session, para.13, (*Selected Decisions 4*, 72).

ISBA/4/C/14, Statement of the President on the work of the Council during the resumed fourth session, paras. 1 and 8, (*Selected Decisions 4*, 75 and 76).

ISBA/4/C/L.3, Draft financial regulations of the International Seabed Authority. Proposed by the Finance Committee.

ISBA/5/C/10, Decision of the Council of the International Seabed Authority concerning the draft financial regulations of the International Seabed Authority, (*Selected Decisions 5*, 46).

ISBA/5/C/11, Statement of the President on the work of the Council at the fifth session, para. 14, (*Selected Decisions 5*, 48-49).

ISBA/5/C/L.3, Draft financial regulations of the International Seabed Authority. Revision of ISBA/4/C/L.3 of 21 August 1998.

ISBA/5/C/L.6, Draft decision of the Council of the International Seabed Authority concerning the draft financial regulations of the International Seabed Authority.

ISBA/16/A/5*-ISBA/16/C/8*, Report of the Finance Committee, para. 23, (*Selected Decisions 16*, 32).

C – DECISION OF THE ASSEMBLY RELATING TO THE OFFICIAL SEAL, FLAG AND EMBLEM OF THE INTERNATIONAL SEABED AUTHORITY

The Assembly of the International Seabed Authority,

Recognizing that it is desirable to approve a distinctive flag and emblem of the International Seabed Authority and to authorize the use of such distinctive emblem for the official seal of the Authority,

Considering that it is necessary to protect the name of the Authority and its distinctive flag, emblem and official seal,

1.   *Resolves* therefore that the designs reproduced in part I of the annex to the present decision shall be the emblem and distinctive design of the International Seabed Authority and shall be used for the official seal of the Authority;

2.   *Resolves also* that the flag of the International Seabed Authority shall be the distinctive emblem reproduced in part II of the annex, centred on a dark blue background;

3.   *Directs* the Secretary-General to draw up regulations concerning the dimensions and proportions of the flag;

4.   *Authorizes* the Secretary-General to adopt a flag code, having in mind the desirability of a regulated use of the flag and the protection of its dignity;

5.   *Recommends*:

(a)   That members of the International Seabed Authority should take such legislative or other appropriate measures as may be necessary to provide for the protection of the emblem, the official seal and the name of the International Seabed Authority, and of abbreviations of that name through the use of its initial letters in order to prevent their use without authorization by the Secretary-General of the International Seabed Authority, and in particular for commercial purposes by means of trade marks or commercial labels;

(b)   That such measures should take effect as soon as practicable but in any event not later than the expiration of two years from the date of adoption of the present resolution;

(c)   That each member of the International Seabed Authority, pending the putting into effect within its territory of any such measures, should use

its best endeavours to provide for the protection of the emblem, name
or initials of the International Seabed Authority, in order to prevent any
use without authorization by the Secretary-General of the International
Seabed Authority, and in particular for commercial purposes by means
of trade marks or commercial labels.

84th meeting
14 August 2002

ANNEX

Part I

Part II

COMMENTARY

The emblem of the International Seabed Authority, which now appears in two principal variants on the official documents of the Authority as well as on the flag, letterheads and publications of the Authority, was created in 1997 and is a modification of the design that had been used by the United Nations for the purposes of the Third United Nations Conference on the Law of the Sea and subsequently by the Office of the Special Representative of the Secretary-General for the Law of the Sea. A different modification of the same design has been formally adopted for use by the International Tribunal for the Law of the Sea. The flag depicts the official seal of the Authority which shows the scales of justice hanging over the waves of the oceans encompassed by a wreath of laurel leaves. Apart from representing justice governing the oceans, the emblem also reflects the strong links between the United Nations Division of Ocean Affairs and the Law of the Sea, the International Tribunal for the Law of the Sea and the Authority.

The official seal, flag and emblem of the Authority were adopted by resolution by the Assembly at its eighty-fourth meeting on 14 August 2002. The decision of the Assembly is contained in document ISBA/8/A/12.

It may be noted that a similar procedure was employed by the United Nations in relation to its emblem and flag. In that case, separate resolutions were adopted on 7 December 1946 relating to the emblem and official seal of the United Nations and on 20 October 1947 relating to the flag of the United Nations.

DOCUMENTARY SOURCES

- ISBA

ISBA/8/A/4, Official seal, flag and emblem of the International Seabed Authority. Report of the Secretary-General.

ISBA/8/A/12, Decision of the Assembly relating to the official seal, flag and emblem of the International Seabed Authority, (*Selected Decisions 8*, 30-31).

ISBA/8/A/13, Statement of the President on the work of the Assembly at the eighth session, para. 15, (*Selected Decisions 8*, 33).

- UNITED NATIONS

Resolution 92 (I), Official Seal and Emblem of the United Nations.

Resolution 167 (II), United Nations Flag.

D – AGREEMENTS REGARDING THE HEADQUARTERS OF THE INTERNATIONAL SEABED AUTHORITY

AGREEMENT BETWEEN THE INTERNATIONAL SEABED AUTHORITY AND THE GOVERNMENT OF JAMAICA REGARDING THE HEADQUARTERS OF THE INTERNATIONAL SEABED AUTHORITY

The International Seabed Authority and the Government of Jamaica,

Having regard to the United Nations Convention on the Law of the Sea of 10 December 1982, which establishes the International Seabed Authority;

Taking into account article 156, paragraph 4, of the Convention, which provides that the seat of the International Seabed Authority shall be in Jamaica;

Recognizing the need to ensure the availability of all necessary facilities to enable the International Seabed Authority to perform its functions as required by the Convention;

Desiring to conclude an agreement for the purpose of regulating, in accordance with the Convention, questions relating to the establishment and functioning of the International Seabed Authority in Jamaica;

Have agreed as follows:

Article 1
Use of terms

For the purposes of this Agreement:

(a) "archives" includes records and correspondence, documents, manuscripts, maps, still and moving pictures, films, computer-based communications and sound recordings belonging to or held by the Authority in Jamaica;

(b) "Authority" means the International Seabed Authority as defined in the Convention;

(c) "competent authorities" means such government, municipal or other authorities in Jamaica as may be appropriate in the context and in accordance with the laws applicable in Jamaica;

(d) "Convention" means the United Nations Convention on the Law of the Sea of 10 December 1982 together with the Agreement relating to the

Implementation of Part XI of the United Nations Convention on the Law of the Sea of 10 December 1982;

(e) "Director-General" means the Director–General of the Enterprise;

(f) "domestic staff" means the persons employed exclusively in the domestic service of the representatives of members of the Authority, of the representatives of observers of the Authority and the officials of the Authority;

(g) "Enterprise" means the organ of the Authority as provided for in the Convention;

(h) "experts" means experts performing missions for the Authority;

(i) "Government" means the Government of Jamaica;

(j) "Headquarters" means the area occupied by the Authority in Jamaica, as specified in article 2;

(k) "laws of Jamaica" means the Constitution of Jamaica, statute law and regulations made pursuant to statutes and includes common law;

(l) "members of the Authority" means all States Parties to the Convention;

(m) "members of the permanent mission" or "members of the permanent observer mission" means the head of the mission and the members of the staff;

(n) "observer State" means a State which enjoys observer status with the Authority;

(o) "observers of the Authority" means States and intergovernmental and non-governmental organizations which enjoy such status with the Authority;

(p) "officials of the Authority" means the Secretary-General and all members of the staff of the Authority, except those who are locally recruited and assigned to hourly rates;

(q) "permanent mission" means a mission of permanent character, representing a member of the Authority;

(r) "permanent observer mission" means a mission of permanent character, representing an observer State;

(s) "Protocol" means the Protocol on the Privileges and Immunities of the Authority;

(t) "representatives of members of the Authority" means delegates, deputy delegates, advisers and any other accredited members of delegations;

(u) "representatives of observer States" means delegates, deputy delegates, advisers and any other accredited members of delegations;

(v) "Secretary-General" means the Secretary-General of the International Seabed Authority or his authorized representative; and

(w) "States Parties" has the same meaning as defined in article 1 of the Convention.

Article 2
The seat of the Authority

1. The seat of the Authority shall be in Jamaica.

2. Jamaica undertakes to grant to the Authority, for the permanent use and occupation by the Authority, such area and facilities as may be specified in supplementary agreements to be concluded for the purpose.

3.   Any building or buildings in Jamaica outside the Headquarters which may, with the concurrence of the Government, be temporarily used for meetings convened by the Authority shall be considered as included in the Headquarters. Requests by the Authority requiring the concurrence of the Government shall not be unreasonably withheld.

Article 3
Legal personality and capacity of the Authority

The Authority shall have international legal personality and such legal capacity as may be necessary for the exercise of its functions and the fulfillment of its purposes in accordance with the Convention; consequently it has, in particular, the capacity:

(a)   To contract;

(b)   To acquire and dispose of immovable and movable property; and

(c)   To be a party to legal proceedings.

Article 4
Law and authority in the Headquarters

1.   The Headquarters shall be under the authority and control of the Authority in accordance with this Agreement.

2.   The Authority shall have the power to adopt regulations, operative within the Headquarters, for the purpose of establishing therein the conditions in all respects necessary for the full and independent exercise of its functions.

3.   The Authority shall promptly inform the Government of regulations adopted by it in accordance with paragraph 2.

4.   Except as otherwise provided in this Agreement and subject to the provisions of paragraphs 2 and 5, the laws of Jamaica shall apply in the Headquarters.

5.   No law of Jamaica which is inconsistent with a regulation of the Authority authorized by paragraph 2 shall, to the extent of such inconsistency, be applicable in the Headquarters.

6.   Any dispute between the Authority and Jamaica as to whether a regulation of the Authority is authorized by paragraph 2, or as to whether a law of Jamaica is inconsistent with any regulation of the Authority authorized by paragraph 2, shall be promptly settled by the procedure set out in article 49. Pending such settlement, the regulation of the Authority shall apply and the law of Jamaica shall be inapplicable in the Headquarters to the extent that the Authority claims it to be inconsistent with the regulation of the Authority.

7.   Except as otherwise provided in this Agreement, the courts of Jamaica or other competent authorities shall have jurisdiction, as provided in applicable laws, over acts done and transactions taking place in the Headquarters.

8.   The courts of Jamaica or other competent authorities, when dealing with cases arising out of or relating to acts done or transactions taking place in the Headquarters, shall take into account the regulations adopted by the Authority under paragraph 2.

9.   The Authority may expel or exclude persons from the Headquarters for violation of its regulations adopted under this article, or for any other proper cause.

10.   Without prejudice to the provisions of this article, the regulations of the competent authorities relating to fire protection and sanitation shall be respected.

Article 5
Inviolability of the Headquarters

1.   The Headquarters shall be inviolable. No officer or official of Jamaica, or other person exercising any public authority within Jamaica, shall enter the Headquarters to perform any duties therein except with the express consent of, or at the request of, the Secretary-General, and under conditions approved by him.

2.   The service of legal process, including the seizure of private property, shall not take place within the Headquarters except with the express consent of, and under conditions approved by, the Secretary-General.

3.   Without prejudice to the provisions of this Agreement, the Authority shall prevent the Headquarters from being used as a refuge from justice by persons who are avoiding arrest under any law of Jamaica, or who are required by the Government for extradition, expulsion or deportation to another country, or who are endeavouring to avoid service of legal process.

4.   In case of fire or other emergency requiring prompt protective action or in the event that the competent authorities have reasonable cause to believe that such an emergency has occurred, the consent of the Secretary-General to entry of the Headquarters by the competent authorities shall be presumed if the Secretary-General cannot be reached in time. Every effort shall be made to seek such consent.

5.   Subject to paragraphs 1 and 2, nothing in this article shall preclude the official delivery by the postal service of Jamaica of letters and documents to the Headquarters.

Article 6
Protection of the Headquarters

1.   The competent authorities shall exercise due diligence to ensure that the tranquillity of the Headquarters and free access thereto are not disturbed by the unauthorized entry of any person or group of persons from outside or by disturbances in its immediate vicinity, and shall provide the Headquarters with such appropriate protection as may be required.

2.   If so requested by the Secretary-General, the competent authorities shall provide a sufficient number of police for the preservation of law and order in the Headquarters, and for the removal therefrom of persons as requested.

3.   The competent authorities shall take all necessary measures to ensure that the Authority shall not be dispossessed of all or any part of the Headquarters without the express consent of the Authority.

Article 7
Vicinity of the Headquarters

1.   The competent authorities shall take all necessary steps to ensure that the amenities of the Headquarters are not prejudiced and that the purposes for which the Headquarters is intended are not obstructed by the use made of the land and buildings in the vicinity of the Headquarters.

2.   The Authority shall take all necessary steps to ensure that the Headquarters is not used for other purposes than those for which it is intended and to ensure that the land and buildings in its vicinity are not unreasonably obstructed.

Article 8
Flag and emblem

The Authority shall be entitled to display its flag and emblem in the Headquarters and on vehicles used for official purposes.

Article 9
Public services in the Headquarters

1.   The competent authorities shall do their utmost to ensure that the Authority shall be provided, on fair and equitable terms but in any case not less favourable than those accorded to the agencies of the Government, with necessary utilities and public services, including but not limited to electricity, water, gas, sewerage, collection of waste, fire protection and local transportation.

2.   In case of any interruption or threatened interruption of any such services, the competent authorities shall consider the needs of the Authority as being of equal importance with those of essential agencies of the Government, and shall take steps accordingly to ensure that the work of the Authority is not prejudiced.

3.   Upon the request of the competent authorities, the Secretary-General shall make suitable arrangements to enable duly authorized representatives of the appropriate public services to inspect, repair, maintain, reconstruct and relocate utilities, conduits, mains and sewers within the Headquarters under conditions which shall not unreasonably disturb the carrying out of the functions of the Authority.

4.   In cases where gas, electricity or water is supplied by the competent authorities, or where the prices thereof are under their control, the Authority shall be supplied at rates which shall not exceed the lowest comparable rates accorded to the agencies of the Government.

5.   The Government shall do its utmost to ensure that the Authority is provided at all times with gasoline or other fuels and lubricating oils for each automobile operated by the Authority on such terms and conditions as may be established for diplomatic missions in Jamaica.

Article 10
Communications facilities

1.   For the purposes of its official communications, the Authority shall enjoy as far as is compatible with international agreements, regulations and arrangements

to which Jamaica is a party, treatment at least as favourable as that which is accorded to diplomatic missions in Jamaica and to international organizations in the matter, *inter alia*, of priorities, rates and taxes applicable to mail and different forms of telecommunications.

2.   The competent authorities shall secure the inviolability of all communications and correspondence directed to the Authority, or to any of the officials of the Authority in the Headquarters, as well as all outgoing communications and correspondence of the Authority, by whatever means or in whatever form transmitted, and they shall be immune from censorship and from any other form of interception or interference with their privacy. Such inviolability shall extend, without limitation by reason of this enumeration, to publications, still and moving pictures, films, computer-based communications and sound or videotape recordings dispatched to or by the Authority.

3.   The Authority shall have the right to use codes and to dispatch and receive its correspondence and other materials by courier or in sealed bags, which shall have the same privileges and immunities as diplomatic couriers and bags.

4.(a)The Authority may establish and operate at the Headquarters:

    (i)   Its own short-wave sending and receiving radio broadcasting facilities, including emergency link equipment which may be used on the same frequencies, within the tolerances prescribed for the broadcasting service by applicable Jamaican regulations, for radiotelegraph, radiotelephone, satellite and similar services;

    (ii) Such other radio facilities as may be specified by supplementary agreement between the Authority and the competent authorities;

  (b) The Authority shall make arrangements for the operation of the services referred to in this paragraph with the International Telecommunication Union, the appropriate agencies of the Government and the appropriate agencies of other affected Governments with regard to all frequencies and similar matters.

5.   The facilities provided for in paragraph 4 may, to the extent necessary for efficient operation, be established and operated outside the Headquarters with the consent of the Government.

6.   If so requested by the Secretary-General, the competent authorities shall provide for the official purposes of the Authority appropriate radio and other telecommunication facilities in conformity with the regulations of the International Telecommunication Union. These facilities may be specified by supplementary agreement between the Authority and the competent authorities.

Article 11
Freedom of publication and broadcasting

The Government recognizes the right of the Authority freely to publish and broadcast within Jamaica in the fulfilment of its purposes set out in the Convention. It is, however, understood that the Authority shall respect any laws of Jamaica or any international agreements to which Jamaica is a party, relating to publications and broadcasting.

Article 12
Freedom of assembly

1.   The Government recognizes the right of the Authority to convene meetings within the Headquarters or, with the concurrence of the Government, elsewhere in Jamaica.

2.   To ensure full freedom of assembly and discussion, the Government shall take all proper steps to guarantee that no impediment is placed in the way of conducting the proceedings of any meeting convened by the Authority.

Article 13
Inviolability of archives

1.   The archives of the Authority, wherever located, shall be inviolable.

2.   The location of the archives of the Authority shall be made known to the competent authorities if it is at a place other than in the Headquarters.

Article 14
Immunity and exemptions of the Authority, its property and assets

1.   The Authority, its property and assets shall enjoy immunity from legal process except to the extent that the Authority expressly waives this immunity in a particular case.

2.   The property and assets of the Authority, wherever located and by whomsoever held, shall be immune from search, requisition, confiscation, expropriation or any other form of seizure by executive or legislative action.

3.   The property and assets of the Authority shall be exempt from restrictions, regulations, controls and moratoria of any nature.

Article 15
Exemption from taxes and customs duties

1.   Within the scope of its official activities, the Authority, its assets and property, its income, and its operations and transactions, authorized by the Convention, shall be exempt from all direct taxation, and goods imported or exported for its official use shall be exempt from all customs duties. The Authority shall not claim exemption from taxes which are no more than charges for services rendered.

2.   When purchases of goods or services of substantial value necessary for the official activities of the Authority are made by or on behalf of the Authority and when the price of such goods or services includes taxes or duties, appropriate measures shall, to the extent practicable, be taken by the Government to grant exemption from such taxes or duties or provide for their reimbursement. With respect to such taxes or duties, the Authority shall at all times enjoy at least the same exemptions as are granted to the heads of diplomatic missions in Jamaica.

3.   Goods imported or purchased under an exemption provided for in this article shall not be sold or otherwise disposed of in the territory of Jamaica, except under conditions agreed with the Government.

Article 16
Financial facilities

1.   Without being subject to any financial controls, regulations or moratoria of any kind, the Authority may freely:

(a)   Purchase any currencies through authorized channels and hold and dispose of them;

(b)   Operate accounts in any currencies;

(c)   Purchase through authorized channels, hold and dispose of, funds, securities and gold;

(d)   Transfer its funds, securities, gold and foreign currencies to or from Jamaica, to or from any other country, or within Jamaica; and

(e)   Raise funds through the exercise of its borrowing power or in any other manner which it deems desirable, except that with respect to the raising of funds within Jamaica, the Authority shall obtain the concurrence of the Government.

2.   The Government shall employ its best endeavours to enable the Authority to obtain the most favourable conditions as regards exchange rates, banking commissions in exchange transactions and the like.

3.   The Authority shall, in exercising its rights under this article, pay due regard to any representations made by the Government in so far as effect can be given to such representations without detriment to the interests of the Authority.

Article 17
Principal office of the Enterprise

The Enterprise shall have its principal office at the seat of the Authority.

Article 18
Legal status of the Enterprise

The Enterprise shall, within the framework of the international legal personality of the Authority, have such legal capacity as is necessary for the exercise of its functions and fulfilment of its purposes and, in particular, the capacity:

(a)   To enter into contracts, joint arrangements or other arrangements, including agreements with States and international organizations;

(b)   To acquire, lease, hold and dispose of immovable and movable property;

(c)   To be a party to legal proceedings.

Article 19
Position of the Enterprise with regard to judicial process

1.   Actions may be brought against the Enterprise in a court of competent jurisdiction in Jamaica.

2.   The property and assets of the Enterprise, wherever located and by whomsoever held, shall be immune from all forms of seizure, attachment or execution before the delivery of final judgement against the Enterprise.

Article 20
Immunity of the property and assets of the Enterprise

1. The property and assets of the Enterprise, wherever located and by whomsoever held, shall be immune from requisition, confiscation, expropriation or any other form of seizure by executive or legislative action.

2. The property and assets of the Enterprise, wherever located and by whomsoever held, shall be free from discriminatory restrictions, regulations, controls and moratoria of any nature.

Article 21
Respect for laws of Jamaica by the Enterprise

The Enterprise shall respect the laws of Jamaica.

Article 22
Rights, privileges and immunities of the Enterprise

1. The Government shall ensure that the Enterprise enjoys all rights, privileges and immunities accorded by it to entities conducting commercial activities in its territory. These rights, privileges and immunities shall be accorded to the Enterprise on no less favourable a basis than that on which they are accorded to entities engaged in similar commercial activities. If special privileges are provided by Jamaica for developing States or their commercial entities, the Enterprise shall enjoy those privileges on a similarly preferential basis.

2. The Government may provide special incentives, rights, privileges and immunities to the Enterprise without the obligation to provide such incentives, rights, privileges and immunities to other commercial entities.

Article 23
Exemption from direct and indirect taxation

The Government and the Enterprise shall enter into special agreements concerning the exemption of the Enterprise from direct and indirect taxation.

Article 24
Financial facilities for the Enterprise

The Enterprise shall have the power to borrow funds and to furnish such collateral or other security as it may determine. Before making a public sale of its obligations in the financial markets or currency of Jamaica, the Enterprise shall obtain the approval of the Government.

Article 25
Waiver of immunity by the Enterprise

The Enterprise may waive any of the privileges and immunities conferred under articles 18, 19, 20, 21, 22 and 23 of this Agreement or in the special agreements provided for in article 51 to such extent and upon such conditions as it may determine.

Article 26
Freedom of access and residence

1.   The Government shall take all necessary measures to facilitate the entry into and residence in Jamaican territory and shall place no impediment in the way of the departure from Jamaican territory of the persons listed below; it shall ensure that no impediment is placed in the way of their transit to or from the Headquarters and shall afford them any necessary protection in transit:

(a)   Representatives of members of the Authority and of observers of the Authority, including alternate representatives, advisers, experts and staff, as well as their spouses, dependent members of their families and domestic staff;

(b)   Officials of the Authority, as well as their spouses, dependent members of their families and domestic staff;

(c)   Officials of the United Nations or of any of its specialized agencies or the International Atomic Energy Agency, attached to the Authority and who have official business with the Authority, as well as their spouses, dependent members of their families and domestic staff;

(d)   Representatives of other organizations with which the Authority has established official relations and who have official business with the Authority as well as their spouses and dependent members of their families;

(e)   Persons on mission for the Authority but who are not officials of the Authority, as well as their spouses and dependent members of their families;

(f)   Representatives of the press, radio, film, television or other information media, who have been accredited to the Authority at its discretion after consultation with the Government;

(g)   All persons invited by the Authority to the Headquarters on official business. The Secretary-General shall communicate the names of such persons to the Government before their intended entry.

2.   This article shall not apply in the case of general interruptions of transportation, which shall be dealt with as provided in article 9, paragraph 2, and shall not impair the effectiveness of generally applicable laws relating to the operations of means of transportation.

3.   Visas, where required for persons referred to in paragraph 1, shall be granted without charge and as promptly as possible.

4.   No activity performed by any person referred to in paragraph 1 in his official capacity with respect to the Authority shall constitute a reason for preventing his entry into or his departure from the territory of Jamaica or for requiring him to leave such territory.

5.   No person referred to in paragraph 1 shall be required by the Government to leave Jamaica save in the event of an abuse of the right of residence, in which case the following procedures shall apply:

(a)   No proceeding shall be instituted to require any such person to leave Jamaica except with the prior approval of the Minister for Foreign Affairs of Jamaica;

(b)   In the case of the representative of a member of the Authority or observer State, such approval shall be given only after consultation with the Government of the member or observer State concerned;

(c) In the case of any other person mentioned in paragraph 1, such approval shall be given only after consultation with the Secretary-General, and if expulsion proceedings are taken against any such person, the Secretary-General shall have the right to appear or to be represented in such proceedings on behalf of the person against whom such proceedings are instituted; and

(d) Officials of the Authority who are entitled to diplomatic privileges and immunities under article 34 shall not be required to leave Jamaica otherwise than in accordance with the customary procedure applicable to members, having comparable rank, of diplomatic missions in Jamaica.

6.   It is understood that persons referred to in paragraph 1 shall not be exempt from the reasonable application of quarantine and other health regulations.

7.   This article shall not prevent the requirement of reasonable evidence to establish that persons claiming the rights granted by this article come within the classes described in paragraph 1.

8.   The Secretary-General and the competent authorities shall, at the request of either of them, consult as to methods of facilitating entry in Jamaica by persons coming from abroad who wish to visit the Headquarters and do not enjoy the privileges and immunities provided by articles 33, 34, 35 and 36.

Article 27
Establishment of missions

1.   A member of the Authority may establish a permanent mission and an observer State may establish a permanent observer mission in Jamaica for the purposes of the representation of that State to the Authority. Such mission shall be accredited to the Authority.

2.   A member of the Authority and an observer State shall notify the Secretary-General of their intention to establish a permanent mission or observer mission.

3.   The Secretary-General shall notify the Government of the intention of a member of the Authority or an observer State to establish a permanent mission or a permanent observer mission upon receipt of such notification.

4.   The permanent mission or the permanent observer mission shall notify the Secretary-General of the names of the members of their missions, as well as the names of spouses and dependent members of their families.

5.   The Secretary-General shall communicate to the Government a list of persons referred to in paragraph 4 and shall revise such list from time to time as may be necessary.

6.   The Government shall provide the members of the permanent mission or the permanent observer mission and their spouses and dependent members of their families with an identity card certifying that they are enjoying the privileges, immunities and facilities specified in this Agreement. This card shall serve to identify the holder in relation to the competent authorities.

Article 28
Privileges and immunities of missions

The permanent mission or the permanent observer mission shall enjoy the same privileges and immunities as are accorded to a diplomatic mission in Jamaica.

Article 29
Privileges and immunities of members of missions

Members of the permanent mission or of the permanent observer mission shall be entitled to the same privileges and immunities as the Government accords to the members, having comparable rank, of a diplomatic mission in Jamaica.

Article 30
Notification

1. The members of the Authority or the observer States shall notify the Authority of the appointment, position and title of the members of the permanent mission or of the observer mission, their arrival, final departure or the termination of their functions with the mission and any other changes affecting their status that occur in the course of their service with the mission.

2. The Authority shall provide the Government with the information referred to in paragraph 1.

Article 31
Assistance by the Authority in respect of privileges and immunities

1. The Authority shall, where necessary, assist the members of the Authority or the observer States, their permanent missions and the members of such mission in securing the enjoyment of the privileges and immunities provided for under this Agreement.

2. The Authority shall, where necessary, assist the Government in securing the discharge of the obligations of the members of the Authority and of the observer States, their missions and members of such missions in respect of the privileges and immunities provided for under this Agreement.

Article 32
Privileges and immunities of the officials of the Authority

1. Without prejudice to article 34, the officials of the Authority, regardless of their nationality and rank, shall enjoy in the territory of Jamaica the following privileges and immunities:

    (a) Immunity from legal process in respect of words spoken and written, and of acts performed by them in their official capacity; such immunity to continue notwithstanding that the persons concerned may have ceased to be officials of the Authority;

    (b) Immunity from personal arrest or detention in relation to acts performed by them in their official capacity;

    (c) Immunity from inspection and seizure of personal and official baggage, except in case of *flagrante delicto*. In such cases the competent authorities shall immediately inform the Secretary-General. Inspections shall, in the case of personal baggage, be conducted only in the presence of the official concerned or his authorized representative, and in the case of official baggage, in the presence of the Secretary-General or his authorized representative;

(d) Exemption from taxation in respect of salaries and emoluments paid or any other form of payment made by the Authority;

(e) Exemption from any form of taxation on income derived by them from sources outside Jamaica;

(f) Exemption from registration fees in respect of their automobiles;

(g) Exemption from immigration restrictions and alien registration procedures;

(h) Exemption from national service obligations, provided that, with respect to Jamaican nationals, such exemption shall be confined to officials of the Authority whose names have, by reason of their duties, been placed upon a list compiled by the Secretary-General and approved by the Government; provided further that, should officials of the Authority, other than those listed, who are Jamaican nationals be called up for national service, the Government shall, upon request of the Secretary-General, grant such temporary deferments in the call-up of such officials of the Authority as may be necessary to avoid interruption of the essential work of the Authority;

(i) The right to purchase petrol free of duty for their vehicles on similar terms as are accorded to members of diplomatic missions in Jamaica;

(j) Exemption for themselves for the purpose of official business from any restrictions on movements and travel inside Jamaica;

(k) In regard to foreign exchange, including holding accounts in foreign currencies, enjoyment of the same facilities as are accorded to members of diplomatic missions in Jamaica;

(l) Enjoyment of the same protection and repatriation facilities as are accorded to members of diplomatic missions in Jamaica, in time of international crisis;

(m) The right to import for personal use, free of duty and other levies, prohibitions and restrictions on imports:

    (i) Their furniture, household and personal effects, in one or more separate shipments, and thereafter to import necessary additions to the same;

    (ii) In accordance with the relevant laws of Jamaica, one automobile, every three years, and in cases where the official is accompanied by dependants, a second automobile on the basis of representations to the Government by the Secretary-General; however, where the Secretary-General and the Government agree, in particular cases, replacement may take place at an earlier date in the event of loss, extensive damage or otherwise; automobiles may be sold in Jamaica after their importation, subject to the laws concerning the payment of customs duties and established diplomatic practice in Jamaica during his or her assignment. After three years such automobiles can be sold without payment of customs duties;

(iii) Reasonable quantities of certain articles including liquor, tobacco, cigarettes and foodstuffs, for personal use or consumption and not for gift or sale. The Authority may establish a commissary for the sale of such articles to the officials of the Authority and members of delegations. A supplementary agreement shall be concluded between the Secretary-General and the Government to regulate the exercise of these rights.

2.   The facilities, privileges and immunities granted to the officials of the Authority in paragraphs 1 (g), 1 (h), 1 (j), and 1 (l) shall extend to their spouses and to dependent family members.

Article 33
Additional privileges and immunities of the Secretary-General and other senior officials of the Authority

1.   The Secretary-General and the Director-General shall be accorded the same privileges and immunities as are accorded to heads of diplomatic missions in Jamaica.

2.   Officials of the Authority at the P-4 level and above, and such additional categories of officials of the Authority as may be designated in an agreement with the Government by the Secretary-General on the ground of the responsibilities of their positions in the Authority regardless of their nationality, shall enjoy the privileges and immunities as the Government accords to the members, having comparable rank, of a diplomatic mission in Jamaica.

Article 34
Application of the Agreement to officials of other international organizations

The provisions of articles 32, 33, paragraph 2, and 36 shall apply to the officials of the United Nations and of its specialized agencies and the International Atomic Energy Agency, attached to the Authority on a continuing basis.

Article 35
Privileges and immunities of experts

1.   Experts, other than the officials of the Authority, while performing the functions assigned to them by the Authority or in the course of their travel to take up those functions or perform those duties, shall enjoy the following privileges, immunities and facilities that are necessary for the effective exercise of their duties:

(a) Immunity from legal process in respect of words spoken and written and all acts performed by them in their official capacity, such immunity to continue notwithstanding that the persons concerned may have ceased to exercise their functions with the Authority;

(b) Immunity from personal arrest or detention in relation to acts performed by them in their official capacity;

(c) Immunity from inspection and seizure of personal and official baggage, except in case of *flagrante delicto*. In such cases the competent authorities shall immediately inform the Secretary-General. Inspections shall, in the case of personal baggage, be conducted only in the presence of the official concerned or his authorized representative, and in the case of official baggage, in the presence of the Secretary-General or his authorized representative;

(d) Exemption from taxation in respect of the salaries and emoluments paid or any other form of payment made by the Authority, provided that nationals of Jamaica may enjoy such exemptions as may be accorded by the Government;

(e) Inviolability of all papers, documents and other official material;

(f) The right, for the purpose of all communications with the Authority, to use codes and to dispatch or receive papers, correspondence or other official material by courier or in sealed bags;

(g) Exemption from immigration restrictions, alien registration and national service obligations;

(h) Enjoyment of the same protection and repatriation facilities as are accorded to the members of diplomatic missions in Jamaica;

(i) The same privileges with respect to currency and exchange restrictions as are accorded to representatives of foreign Governments on temporary official missions.

2.   The facilities, privileges and immunities granted to experts in paragraphs 1 (g) and (h) shall extend to their spouses and dependent family members.

Article 36
Waiver of immunity of the officials of the Authority and experts

Privileges and immunities are granted to the officials of the Authority and experts in the interests of the Authority and not for their own personal benefit. The Secretary-General shall have the right and the duty to waive the immunity of any official of the Authority or expert in any case where, in his opinion, the immunity would impede the course of justice and can be waived without prejudice to the interests of the Authority. In the case of the Secretary-General, the Council shall have the right to waive the immunity.

Article 37
List of officials of the Authority and experts

The Secretary-General shall communicate to the Government a list of persons referred to in articles 32, 33, 34 and 35 and shall revise such list from time to time as may be necessary.

Article 38
Abuse of privilege or immunity

1.   The Secretary-General shall take every precaution to ensure that no abuse of a privilege or immunity conferred by this Agreement shall occur and, for this

purpose, the Council shall adopt rules and regulations as may be deemed necessary and expedient for officials of the Authority.

2.   Should the Government consider that an abuse of a privilege or immunity conferred by this Agreement has occurred, the Secretary-General shall, upon request, consult with the Government to determine whether any such abuse has occurred. If such consultations fail to achieve a result satisfactory to the Secretary-General and to the Government, the matter shall be determined in accordance with the procedure set out in article 48.

Article 39
Identity card

The Government shall provide the officials of the Authority and the experts with an identity card certifying that they are enjoying the privileges, immunities and facilities specified in this Agreement. This card shall also serve to identify the holder in relation to the competent authorities.

Article 40
Cooperation with the competent authorities

The Authority shall cooperate at all times with the competent authorities to facilitate the proper administration of justice, secure the observance of police regulations and avoid the occurrence of any abuse in connection with the privileges, immunities and facilities mentioned in this Agreement.

Article 41
Respect for the laws of Jamaica

Without prejudice to the privileges, immunities and facilities accorded by this Agreement, it is the duty of all persons enjoying such privileges, immunities and facilities to respect the laws of Jamaica. They also have the duty not to interfere in the internal affairs of Jamaica.

Article 42
Laissez-passer

1.   The Government shall recognize and accept laissez-passer issued to the officials of the Authority as a valid travel document equivalent to a passport.

2.   The Government shall recognize and accept certificates issued to experts and other persons travelling on the business of the Authority. The Government agrees to issue any required visas based on such certificates.

3.   Applications for visas from the holders of laissez-passer, when accompanied by a certificate that they are travelling on the business of the Authority, shall be dealt with as speedily as possible.

4.   Similar facilities to those specified in paragraph 3 shall be accorded to experts and other persons who, though not holders of laissez-passer, have a certificate that they are travelling on the business of the Authority.

Article 43
Social security and pension funds

1.   The United Nations Joint Staff Pension Fund shall, when the Authority is a member, enjoy legal capacity in Jamaica and shall enjoy the same exemptions, privileges and immunities as the Authority itself.

2.   The Authority shall be exempt from all compulsory contributions to, and officials of the Authority shall not be required by the Government to participate in, any social security scheme of Jamaica.

3.   The Government shall make such provision as may be necessary to enable any official of the Authority who is not afforded social security coverage by the Authority to participate, if the Authority so requests, in any social security scheme of Jamaica, to the extent that such scheme exists. The Authority shall, insofar as possible, arrange, under conditions to be agreed upon, for the participation in any Jamaican social security system, to the extent that such a system exists, of those locally recruited members of its staff who do not participate in the United Nations Joint Staff Pension Fund or to whom the Authority does not grant social security protection at least equivalent to that offered under the laws of Jamaica.

Article 44
Responsibility, liability and insurance

1.   Jamaica shall not incur by reason of the location of the Headquarters within its territory any international responsibility for acts or omissions of the Authority or of its officials acting or abstaining from acting within the scope of their functions, other than the international responsibility which Jamaica would incur as a member of the Authority.

2.   Without prejudice to its immunities under this Agreement, the Authority shall carry insurance to cover liability for any injury or damage arising from activities of the Authority in Jamaica or from its use of the Headquarters that may be suffered by persons other than the officials of the Authority, or by the Government. To this end, the competent authorities shall make every reasonable effort to secure for the Authority, at reasonable rates, insurance coverage permitting claims to be submitted directly to the insurer by parties suffering injury or damage. Such claims and liability shall, without prejudice to the privileges and immunities of the Authority, be governed by the laws of Jamaica.

Article 45
Security

Without prejudice to the performance of its functions by the Authority in a normal and unrestricted manner, the Government may take every preventive measure to preserve the national security of Jamaica after consultation with the Secretary-General.

Article 46
Responsibility of the Government

Whenever this Agreement imposes obligations on the competent authorities, the ultimate responsibility for the fulfilment of such obligations shall rest with the Government.

Article 47
Special agreement relating to the Enterprise

The provisions of this Agreement relating to the Enterprise may be supplemented by a special agreement to be concluded between the Enterprise and the Government in accordance with Annex IV, article 13, paragraph 1, of the Convention.

Article 48
Settlement of disputes

1. The Authority shall make suitable provisions for the proper settlement of:
   (a) Disputes arising out of contracts, or disputes of a private law character to which the Authority is a party;
   (b) Disputes involving an official of the Authority or any person who by reason of his official position enjoys immunity, if such immunity has not been waived.

2. Any dispute between the Authority and the competent authorities concerning the interpretation or application of this Agreement or of any supplementary agreement, or any question affecting the Headquarters or the relationship between the Authority and the Government which is not settled by consultation, negotiation or other agreed mode of settlement within three months following such a request by one of the parties to the dispute, shall be referred, at the request of either party to the dispute, for a final and binding decision to a panel of three arbitrators: one to be nominated by the Secretary-General, one to be nominated by the Government. If either or both of the nominations are not made within three months following the request for arbitration, the President of the International Tribunal for the Law of the Sea shall proceed to make the appointment. The third arbitrator, who shall be the chairman of the panel, shall be chosen by the first two arbitrators. Should the first two arbitrators fail to agree upon the appointment of the third arbitrator within three months following the nomination or appointment of the first two arbitrators, such third arbitrator shall be chosen by the President of the International Tribunal for the Law of the Sea at the request of the Authority or the Government.

Article 49
Application of the Agreement

This Agreement shall apply irrespective of whether the Government maintains diplomatic relations with a member of the Authority or an observer State. It shall be applied to all persons entitled to privileges and immunities under this Agreement, regardless of their nationality and irrespective of whether their State grants a similar privilege or immunity to diplomatic agents or nationals of Jamaica.

Article 50
Relationship between the Agreement and the Protocol

The provisions of this Agreement shall be complementary to the provisions of the Protocol. Insofar as any provision of this Agreement and any provisions of the Protocol relate to the same subject matter, the two provisions shall, wherever possible, be treated as complementary, so that both provisions shall be applicable and neither shall narrow the effect of the other; but in any case of conflict, the provisions of this Agreement shall prevail.

Article 51
Supplementary agreements

1.   The Authority and the Government may enter into such supplementary agreements as may be necessary.

2.   If and to the extent that the Government shall enter into any agreement with any intergovernmental organization containing terms or conditions more favourable to that organization than similar terms or conditions of this Agreement, the Government shall extend such more favourable terms or conditions to the Authority, by means of a supplemental agreement.

3.   Paragraph 2 shall not apply to any terms or conditions granted by the Government pursuant to any agreement establishing a customs union, free-trade area or economic integration organization.

Article 52
Amendments

Consultations with respect to amendments to this Agreement shall be entered into at the request of either party. Any such amendment shall be by mutual consent and shall be expressed in an exchange of letters or an agreement concluded by the Authority and the Government.

Article 53
Termination of the Agreement

This Agreement shall cease to be in force by mutual consent of the Authority and the Government, except for such provisions as may be applicable in connection with the orderly termination of the operations of the Authority at its Headquarters in Jamaica and the disposal of its property therein.

Article 54
Final provisions

1.   This Agreement shall enter into force on its approval by the Assembly of the Authority and the Government of Jamaica.

2.   This Agreement shall be applied provisionally by the Authority and the Government upon signature by the Secretary-General of the Authority and on behalf of the Government of Jamaica.

SUPPLEMENTARY AGREEMENT BETWEEN THE INTERNATIONAL SEABED AUTHORITY AND THE GOVERNMENT OF JAMAICA REGARDING THE HEADQUARTERS OF THE INTERNATIONAL SEABED AUTHORITY AND THE USE OF THE JAMAICA CONFERENCE CENTRE COMPLEX

In pursuance of the Agreement between the International Seabed Authority (hereinafter called "the Authority") and the Government of Jamaica (hereinafter called "the Government") regarding the headquarters of the Authority done at Kingston, Jamaica, on the 26th day of August 1999 (hereinafter called "the Headquarters Agreement");

Considering that, pursuant to article 2 of the Headquarters Agreement, the Government undertook to grant to the Authority, for the permanent use and occupation of the Authority, such area and facilities as may be specified in supplementary agreements concluded for the purpose;

Desiring therefore to conclude such an agreement, supplementing the Headquarters Agreement, in order to regulate the terms under which the Authority may use and occupy its headquarters and setting out the terms and conditions under which the Authority shall have the use of facilities of the Jamaica Conference Centre for the purpose of its meetings;

Now therefore, the Parties hereto agree as follows:

Article 1
Use of terms

1.   The terms used in this Agreement shall have the same meaning as those in the Headquarters Agreement.

2.   This Agreement includes the annexes to this Agreement, which shall be an integral part hereof.

Article 2
Purpose and scope

This Agreement serves to set out the terms and conditions governing the use and occupancy by the Authority of the premises granted by the Government as the permanent headquarters of the Authority in Kingston, Jamaica, and the use of the Jamaica Conference Centre by the Authority for the purposes of its activities.

Article 3
Grant of premises

The Government hereby grants to the Authority for a period of 99 years free of rent and all other charges except as provided for in this Agreement all the premises more particularly described in annex I hereto (hereinafter referred to as "the Premises") for use as the permanent headquarters of the Authority in Kingston, Jamaica, together with a right of access to and from the Premises, the right in common with other tenants of the building within which the Premises are located to the use of common facilities, elevators, fire systems, air conditioning, parking lot and other common areas of such building. In the event that additional space in the building within which the Premises are located is required for use and occupation by the Authority, annex I shall be amended and the provisions of this Agreement shall apply *mutatis mutandis* thereto.

Article 4
Use and occupancy of the Premises

1.   The Premises shall be used and occupied by the Authority as its permanent headquarters in Kingston, Jamaica.

2.   The Authority shall have the right to quiet and peaceful occupancy and use of the Premises, without undue interruptions and disturbances, for the conduct of its official activities. The Government shall make every effort to ensure that the use of the immediate vicinity of the Premises does not obstruct the usefulness of the Premises to the Authority.

3.   The Authority shall take all necessary steps to ensure that the Premises are not used for purposes other than those for which it is intended and to ensure that the land and buildings in its vicinity are not unreasonably obstructed.

Article 5
Operating costs of the Premises

1.   During the term herein granted, the Authority shall contribute a proportionate amount, commensurate with the area occupied by the Authority, of the costs incurred by the Government in respect of the maintenance and normal wear and tear of the building within which the Premises are located, as shown in annex II hereto (hereinafter called "the Monthly Maintenance Contribution").

2.   The Monthly Maintenance Contribution shall be payable at the end of each month and shall constitute the sole contribution by the Authority towards the costs of its use and occupation of the Premises. The Authority shall be directly responsible for the payment of electricity consumption in the Premises occupied by the Authority.

3.   The Monthly Maintenance Contribution shall be reviewed three years from the effective date of this Agreement and every two years thereafter. In the light of the review, the Government and the Authority may make such adjustments to annex II as may be necessary by mutual agreement. If there are special circumstances which make a review necessary before the expiration of two years from the date of the last

review, either Party may request a review of the Monthly Maintenance Contribution at any time in accordance with the provisions of article 17.

Article 6
Alterations, fixtures, installations and maintenance of the Premises

1.   The Government shall, at its expense, maintain the Premises, the lands and building within which the Premises are located, in good condition of repair and maintenance, and shall keep and maintain the exterior of said lands and buildings and the common areas, including elevators, fire protection systems and air conditioning, in good, attractive and operating condition.

2.   The Government shall, at its expense, provide the Premises with water, electricity and any other services and facilities required by the Authority to carry out its functions. The elevator, air conditioning and cleaning services shall be provided as indicated in annex II.

3.   The Government shall be responsible, at its own expense, for restoration, renovation and major repairs or extensive maintenance to the Premises including structural repairs and replacements to the buildings, installations, fixtures and equipment, such as building control equipment, air-conditioning equipment, pipes, plumbing and electrical wiring.

4.   The Government shall, if so requested by the Secretary-General, facilitate the installation of equipment referred to in article 10, paragraph 6, of the Headquarters Agreement in order for the Authority to operate its own telecommunications system.

5.   The Authority will report any necessary repairs that are the responsibility of the Government to the competent authority, who shall, on behalf of the Government, take prompt and effective action in response.

6.   The Authority may, upon notice to the competent authorities, at its own expense, attach fixtures and make alterations and installations on the Premises for its own purposes. In any case involving structural alterations the Authority shall do so with the consent of the competent authorities and taking into consideration the building regulations of the host country.

7.   The equipment, fixtures or installations erected or installed by the Authority, except for immovable fixtures or installations, shall not become part of the realty and may be removed by the Authority at any time or upon expiration of this Agreement or any renewal thereof, except for those improvements which the Authority shall, upon request by the Government giving thirty days' notice to the Authority, agree to sell to the Government; in which case the Government shall reimburse the Authority the cost thereof at the prevailing book value. Provided that upon removal of the equipment, fixtures or installations erected by the Authority, the Authority shall, if requested by the Government, restore the Premises to the same condition as that existing at the time of taking possession of the same, reasonable and ordinary wear and tear and damage by the elements or by circumstances over which the Authority has no control excepted.

Article 7
Damage to or destruction of the Premises

1. The Authority shall not be responsible for restoration or reconstruction of the Premises in case of damage or destruction by fire or any other external cause, including force majeure.

2. In the event of total destruction of the Premises or the building of which the Premises form a part due to fire, force majeure or any other cause, this Agreement, including the payment obligations assumed by the Authority hereunder, shall immediately terminate. In such event, the Government shall provide the Authority with other suitable premises.

3. In the event of partial destruction of the Premises or the building of which the Premises form a part, the Authority shall have the option to continue with the Agreement if the Government within 60 days of such occurrence satisfies the Authority that adequate measures have been taken or are proposed to restore the Premises within a reasonable time. Should the Authority elect to remain on Premises rendered partially untenable, it shall have the right to a proportionate rebate or reduction of the payments made or due to the Government pursuant to this Agreement.

Article 8
Access to Premises

Without prejudice to article 5 of the Headquarters Agreement, the Authority shall, upon request, enable duly authorized representatives of the competent authorities of the Government to enter the Premises to inspect the buildings, facilities and installations at the Premises under conditions which shall not unreasonably disturb the carrying out of the functions of the Authority, with due notice given and subject to prior approval of the Secretary-General.

Article 9
Use of the Centre

1. The Government hereby agrees to make available to the Authority whenever necessary and upon request in writing at least 30 days in advance, the Jamaica Conference Centre (hereafter called "the Centre"), for the purpose of holding meetings, conferences, consultations, scheduled programmes and any other activities related to the functions of the Authority.

2. Rates applied to the Authority for its use of the Centre shall not be less favourable than those applicable to the Government, its agencies or any other local organizations or bodies.

Article 10
Facilities, services and maintenance in the Centre

1. For purpose of giving effect to the provisions of paragraph 1 of article 9 hereof, the Government shall during the user period provide to the Authority the following facilities:

(a) Full and exclusive use of the conference rooms, dining facilities and other amenities;

(b) Post office, telephone and fax facilities;

(c) Parking facilities.

2.   During the user period, the Government shall maintain the facilities described in paragraph 1 in good order and condition and the Government shall provide:

(a) Maintenance services, including ventilation and air conditioning, in respect of the Centre;

(b) All utilities and other services including water, electricity, air conditioning and cooking gas;

(c) Maintenance of the fire equipment and fire detection system;

(d) Maintenance and repair of kitchen equipment;

(e) Maintenance and repair of the electronic equipment;

(f) Maintenance and repair of air-conditioning equipment;

(g) Janitorial services;

(h) Security services;

(i) Parking facilities;

(j) Insurance coverage as provided in article 11.

Article 11
Insurance

1.   During the term of this Agreement or any extension thereof, the Government shall in respect of the Premises and, during the user period, the Centre, procure and maintain at its expense fire insurance with extended coverage endorsement; provided, however, that the Government shall not be obligated to insure the fixtures, furnishings and other equipment owned and installed in the Premises by the Authority.

2.   The Government shall carry adequate public liability insurance covering its ownership of the Centre and the Premises, and shall carry adequate public liability insurance covering the lands and buildings, parking lot, sidewalk and other common areas.

3.   The Government shall provide the Authority with proof that the insurance coverage provided for in this article has been obtained.

4.   In case of loss or damage or destruction of the Premises or the Centre by fire or any other cause whatsoever, the Government or its insurer, agents or assignees shall not look to the Authority or its agents or employees for reimbursement who shall not have any liability or financial responsibility in this regard, except where attributable to gross negligence or wilful default of the Authority.

5.   During the term of this Agreement or any extension thereof, the Authority shall carry adequate insurance to cover its liability as provided in article 44 of the Headquarters Agreement.

Article 12
Interruption or curtailment of services

1.   In the event of interruption or curtailment, whether due to strikes, mechanical difficulties or other causes, of any services maintained or required to

be maintained in the Premises or the Centre, the Government undertakes to take such measures as may be necessary to restore the services without undue delay. The Authority shall have a right to a proportionate abatement or reduction of the use and occupancy costs herein provided during the period of such interruptions or curtailment.

2.   The Authority shall notify the Government of any such interruption or curtailment and the Parties shall consult with a view to determining the extent of the interruption or curtailment and the steps required to restore the services.

Article 13
Privileges and immunities

Nothing contained in this Agreement shall be construed as a derogation from or a waiver, express or implied, of any of the privileges and immunities of the Authority. Furthermore, this Agreement shall be subject to and shall be construed and applied in a manner consistent with the Headquarters Agreement.

Article 14
Responsibility for the obligations on the competent authority

1.   Whenever this Agreement imposes obligations on the competent authorities, the responsibility for the fulfilment of such obligations shall lie with the Government.

2.   Communications concerning the Premises and use of the Centre will be between the Authority and the Government. Communications may be addressed to the Ministry of Foreign Affairs and Foreign Trade, including requests regarding services or equipment, repairs and maintenance. Such communications and requests shall be deemed to have been communicated to the Government.

Article 15
Consultations

At the request of either the Government or the Authority, consultations may be held on any matter related to the use and management of the Premises or the Centre that may affect the interest of the Authority, with a view to reaching a mutually satisfactory agreement.

Article 16
Settlement of disputes

Any dispute between the Government and the Authority concerning the interpretation or application of this Agreement shall be settled in accordance with article 48, paragraph 2, of the Headquarters Agreement.

Article 17
Revision and amendment

This Agreement, including the annexes, may be revised or amended at any time upon the request of either of the Parties, subject to mutual consultation and mutual consent to any such revisions or amendments.

Article 18
Termination

1.   This Agreement may be terminated by mutual consent by either party giving 90 days' advance notice of its intention to terminate to the other. Such consent shall not be unreasonably withheld. In such a case, either party may request consultations.

2.   Upon termination of this Agreement, the Authority shall surrender the Premises to the Government in good condition and repair, ordinary wear and tear, the elements, force majeure and loss through fire and other insurable risks excepted.

Article 19
Entry into force

1.   This Agreement shall enter into force on its approval by the Assembly of the Authority and the Government of Jamaica.

2.   This Agreement shall be applied provisionally by the Authority and the Government upon signature by the Secretary-General of the Authority and on behalf of the Government of Jamaica.

IN WITNESS WHEREOF the undersigned, being duly authorized representatives of the International Seabed Authority and the Government of Jamaica, have signed the present Agreement.

SIGNED this seventeenth day of December 2003 (two thousand and three) at Kingston, Jamaica, in two originals in the English language.

FOR THE INTERNATIONAL	FOR THE GOVERNMENT
SEABED AUTHORITY:	OF JAMAICA:
[Signature] **Satya N. Nandan**	[Signature] **Rt. Hon. K. D. Knight**
Secretary-General	Minister of Foreign Affairs and
	Foreign Trade

(Annexes not reproduced)

COMMENTARY

The Headquarters Agreement

Article 156, paragraph 4, of the 1982 Convention provides that the seat of the Authority shall be in Jamaica. When the Secretariat of the Authority became operational in 1996, it took over the premises formerly occupied by the Kingston Office for the Law of the Sea, established by the United Nations to service the Preparatory Commission. For that purpose, there had been in effect an agreement between the Government of Jamaica and the United Nations relating to the use of the premises.

At its eighth meeting, on 11 November 1996, the Council formally requested the Secretary-General to negotiate with the Government of Jamaica an agreement regarding the headquarters of the Authority, taking into account the draft of such an agreement prepared by the Preparatory Commission (LOS/PCN/WP.47/Rev.2). The Council also decided that such negotiations would be under its guidance (ISBA/C/11). Following negotiations between the Secretary-General and the Government of Jamaica, a draft headquarters agreement (ISBA/3/A/L.3-ISBA/3/C/L.3 and Corr.1) was submitted for consideration of the Council at the third session of the Authority (1997). In the light of concerns expressed by some delegations, it was not possible to resolve all outstanding issues, particularly with respect to article 2 of the draft agreement, and the matter was deferred to the fourth session. At the fourth session, the matter was further deferred to the fifth session, at which time the Secretary-General presented a report to the Assembly on considerations relating to an offer by the Government of Jamaica for the headquarters of the Authority (ISBA/5/A/4 and Add.1). That report was considered further by the Finance Committee, which recommended that the Assembly approve the recommendations of the Secretary-General contained in the report (ISBA/5/C/7). Having considered the recommendations of the Finance Committee, the Council decided, on 24 August 1999, to recommend to the Assembly that it approve the Headquarters Agreement contained in document ISBA/3/A/L.3-ISBA/3/C/L.3 and Corr.1.

The headquarters agreement between the International Seabed Authority and the Government of Jamaica was approved by the Assembly at its sixty-seventh meeting, on 25 August 1999. At that time, the Assembly also accepted the offer of the Government of Jamaica for the use of the Authority's existing premises (i.e. that formerly occupied by the Kingston Office for the Law of the Sea) for the use and occupation of the Authority as its permanent headquarters. The decision of the Assembly approving the headquarters agreement is contained in document ISBA/5/A/11. At the sixty-eighth meeting of the Assembly, on 26 August 1999, in a formal ceremony, the Headquarters Agreement was signed by the Secretary-General, on behalf of the Authority, and by the Minister of Foreign Affairs of Jamaica, the Honourable Seymour Mullings, on behalf of the Government of Jamaica.

The provisions of the Headquarters Agreement and the provisions of the Protocol on the Privileges and Immunities of the International Seabed Authority (ISBA/4/A/8), adopted by the Assembly in 1998, are complementary.

The Supplementary Agreement

In the decision approving the Headquarters Agreement, the Assembly requested the Secretary-General to negotiate with the Government of Jamaica, pursuant to article 2 of the Headquarters Agreement, a supplementary agreement concerning the use and occupation of the permanent headquarters. In October 1999, the Secretary-General invited the Government of Jamaica to commence as soon as possible the negotiations for that purpose. It was not possible to reach an early agreement on the parameters of the proposed supplementary agreement and a number of problems emerged which made progress difficult to achieve. At the ninth session, in 2003, the Assembly reiterated its concern over the long delay in negotiating the Supplementary Agreement and urged the Secretary-General and the Government of Jamaica to renew their efforts to conclude an agreement as soon as possible. This was achieved by November 2003. Subsequently, at a ceremony at the headquarters of the Authority in Kingston on 17 December 2003, the Supplementary Agreement was signed by the Secretary-General, on behalf of the Authority, and by the Hon. K. D. Knight, Minister of Foreign Affairs and Foreign Trade, on behalf of the Government of Jamaica.

In accordance with its article 19, the Supplementary Agreement had been applied provisionally since its signature by both parties. At its ninety-fifth meeting on 2 June 2004, upon the decision of the Council acting on recommendation of the Finance Committee, the Assembly approved the Supplementary Agreement (ISBA/10/A/11), which entered into force on that same date.

The text of the Supplementary Agreement is in the annex to the document ISBA/10/A/2-ISBA/10/C/2.

DOCUMENTARY SOURCES

The Headquarters Agreement

- PREPARATORY COMMISSION
LOS/PCN/WP.47/Rev.2, Final draft Agreement between the International
    Seabed Authority and the Government of Jamaica regarding the
    Headquarters of the International Seabed Authority, reproduced in:
    LOS/PCN/153, Vol. V, p. 97-125.
- ISBA
ISBA/A/L.7/Rev.1, Statement of the President on the work of the Assembly
    during the third part of its first session, paras. 16 to 18, (*Selected
    Decisions 1/2/3*, 9).
ISBA/3/A/4, Report of the Secretary-General of the International Seabed
    Authority under article 166, paragraph 4, of the United Nations
    Convention on the Law of the Sea, paras. 13 and 24-26, (*Selected
    Decisions 1/2/3*, 47 and 51).
ISBA/3/A/11, Statement of the President on the work of the Assembly during
    the resumed third session, para. 12, (*Selected Decisions 1/2/3*, 63).
ISBA/3/A/L.3-ISBA/3/C/L.3 and Corr. 1, Agreement between the
    International Seabed Authority and the Government of Jamaica
    regarding the headquarters of the International Seabed Authority.
ISBA/3/A/L.4, Statement of the President on the work of the Assembly
    during the third session, paras. 1 and 9, (*Selected Decisions 1/2/3*,
    43 and 44).
ISBA/4/A/9, Statement of the President on the work of the Assembly
    during the fourth session, paras. 14 and 15 and annex "Letter dated
    10 March 1998 from the Minister of Foreign Affairs and Foreign
    Trade of Jamaica to the Secretary-General of the International Seabed
    Authority, (*Selected Decisions 4*, 51-52).
ISBA/4/A/11, Report of the Secretary-General of the International
    Seabed Authority under article 166, paragraph 4, of the United
    Nations Convention on the Law of the Sea, paras. 17-20, (*Selected
    Decisions 4*, 55).
ISBA/4/A/18, Statement of the President on the work of the Assembly
    during the resumed fourth session, paras. 6 to 8 and 15, (*Selected
    Decisions 4*, 65-66).
ISBA/5/A/1 and Corr.1, Report of the Secretary-General of the
    International Seabed Authority under article 166, paragraph 4, of
    the United Nations Convention on the Law of the Sea, paras. 6 to 8
    and 52, (*Selected Decisions 5*, 1-2 and 11).
ISBA/5/A/4, Considerations relating to the offer by the Government of
    Jamaica concerning the location of the permanent headquarters of

the Authority. Report of the Secretary-General, (*Selected Decisions 5*, 12-16).

ISBA/5/A/4/Add. 1, Considerations relating to the offer by the Government of Jamaica concerning the location of the permanent headquarters of the Authority. Report of the Secretary-General. Addendum, (*Selected Decisions 5*, 16-17).

ISBA/5/A/8-ISBA/5/C/7, Proposed budget of the International Seabed Authority for 2000 and related matters. Report of the Finance Committee, para. 17, (*Selected Decisions 5*, 20).

ISBA/5/A/11, Decision of the Assembly of the International Seabed Authority relating to the Headquarters of the International Seabed Authority, (*Selected Decisions 5*, 21-38).

ISBA/5/A/14, Statement of the President on the work of the Assembly at the fifth session, paras. 20-22, (*Selected Decisions 5*, 42).

ISBA/C/11, Decision of the Council of the International Seabed Authority concerning the headquarters agreement between the International Seabed Authority and the Government of Jamaica, (*Selected Decisions 1/2/3*, 37-38).

ISBA/C/L.3, Statement of the President Pro Tem on the work of the Council during the resumed second session, para. 11, (*Selected Decisions 1/2/3*, 39-40).

ISBA/3/C/11, Statement of the President on the work of the Council during the resumed third session, para. 11, (*Selected Decisions 1/2/3*, 74).

ISBA/3/C/L.4, Statement of the President on the work of the Council during the third session, para. 10, (*Selected Decisions 1/2/3*, 66).

ISBA/4/C/5, Statement of the President on the work of the Council during the first part of the fourth session, para. 11, (*Selected Decisions 4*, 72).

ISBA/4/C/14, Statement of the President on the work of the Council during the resumed fourth session, para. 1, (*Selected Decisions 4*, 75).

ISBA/5/C/9, Decision of the Council of the International Seabed Authority relating to the headquarters of the International Seabed Authority, (*Selected Decisions 5*, 45-46).

ISBA/5/C/11, Statement of the President on the work of the Council at the fifth session, paras. 7-9, (*Selected Decisions 5*, 47-48).

The Supplementary Agreement

- ISBA

ISBA/7/A/2, Report of the Secretary-General of the International Seabed Authority under article 166, paragraph 4, of the United Nations Convention on the Law of the Sea, para. 10, (*Selected Decisions 7*, 5-6).

ISBA/7/A/7, Statement of the President on the work of the Assembly at the seventh session, para. 12, (*Selected Decisions 7*, 18).

ISBA/8/A/5, Report of the Secretary-General of the International Seabed Authority under article 166, paragraph 4, of the United Nations Convention on the Law of the Sea, paras. 11-21, (*Selected Decisions 8*, 11-13).

ISBA/8/A/5/Add.1, Report of the Secretary-General of the International Seabed Authority under article 166, paragraph 4, of the United Nations Convention on the Law of the Sea. Addendum, (*Selected Decisions 8*, 23-24).

ISBA/8/A/13, Statement of the President on the work of the Assembly at the eighth session, para. 9, (*Selected Decisions 8*, 32).

ISBA/9/A/3, Report of the Secretary-General of the International Seabed Authority under article 166, paragraph 4, of the United Nations Convention on the Law of the Sea, paras. 11-14, (*Selected Decisions 9, 2-3*).

ISBA/9/A/9, Statement of the President on the work of the Assembly at the ninth session, para. 8, (*Selected Decisions 9*, 21).

ISBA/10/A/2-ISBA/10/C/2, Supplementary Agreement between the International Seabed Authority and the Government of Jamaica regarding the headquarters of the International Seabed Authority and the use of the Jamaica Conference Centre complex, (*Selected Decisions 10*, 1-10).

ISBA/10/A/6-ISBA/10/C/7, Report of the Finance Committee, paras. 19-20, (*Selected Decisions 10*, 53).

ISBA/10/A/11, Decision of the Assembly of the International Seabed Authority relating to the Supplementary Agreement between the International Seabed Authority and the use of the Jamaica Conference Centre complex, (*Selected Decisions 10*, 55).

ISBA/10/A/12, Statement of the President on the work of the Assembly at the tenth session, paras. 8 and 20-21, (*Selected Decisions 10*, 57 and 59).

ISBA/10/C/5, Decision of the Council of the International Seabed Authority relating to the Supplementary Agreement between the International Seabed Authority and the Government of Jamaica regarding the headquarters of the Jamaican Conference Centre complex, (*Selected Decisions 10*, 68).

ISBA/10/C/10, Statement of the President on the work of the Council at the tenth session, para. 9, (*Selected Decisions 10*, 71).

ISBA/11/A/4 and Corr.1, Report of the Secretary-General of the International Seabed Authority under article 166, paragraph 4, of the United Nations Convention on the Law of the Sea, paras. 11-12, (*Selected Decisions 11*, 2-3).

E – PROTOCOL ON THE PRIVILEGES AND IMMUNITIES OF THE INTERNATIONAL SEABED AUTHORITY

The States Parties to this Protocol,

Considering that the United Nations Convention on the Law of the Sea establishes the International Seabed Authority,

Recalling that article 176 of the United Nations Convention on the Law of the Sea provides that the Authority shall have international legal personality and such legal capacity as may be necessary for the exercise of its functions and the fulfilment of its purposes,

Noting that article 177 of the United Nations Convention on the Law of the Sea provides that the Authority shall enjoy in the territory of each State Party to the Convention the privileges and immunities set forth in section 4, subsection G of Part XI of the Convention and that the privileges and immunities of the Enterprise shall be those set forth in annex IV, article 13,

Recognizing that certain additional privileges and immunities are necessary for the exercise of the functions of the International Seabed Authority,

Have agreed as follows:

Article 1
Use of terms

For the purposes of this Protocol:

(a) "Authority" means the International Seabed Authority;

(b) "Convention" means the United Nations Convention on the Law of the Sea of 10 December 1982;

(c) "Agreement" means the Agreement relating to the Implementation of Part XI of the United Nations Convention on the Law of the Sea of 10 December 1982. In accordance with the Agreement, its provisions and Part XI of the Convention are to be interpreted and applied together as a single instrument; this Protocol and references in this Protocol to the Convention are to be interpreted and applied accordingly;

(d) "Enterprise" means the organ of the Authority as provided for in the Convention;

(e) "member of the Authority" means:

(i) any State Party to the Convention; and

(ii) any State or entity which is a member of the Authority on a provisional basis pursuant to paragraph 12 (a) of section 1 of the annex to the Agreement;

(f) "representatives" means representatives, alternate representatives, advisers, technical experts and secretaries of the delegations;

(g) "Secretary-General" means the Secretary-General of the International Seabed Authority.

Article 2
General provision

Without prejudice to the legal status, privileges and immunities accorded to the Authority and the Enterprise set forth in section 4, subsection G, of Part XI and Annex IV, article 13, of the Convention respectively, each State Party to this Protocol shall accord to the Authority and its organs, the representatives of members of the Authority, officials of the Authority and experts on mission for the Authority such privileges and immunities as are specified in this Protocol.

Article 3
Legal personality of the Authority

The Authority shall possess legal personality. It shall have the legal capacity:
(a) to contract;
(b) to acquire and dispose of immovable and movable property;
(c) to be a party in legal proceedings.

Article 4
Inviolability of the premises of the Authority

The premises of the Authority shall be inviolable.

Article 5
Financial facilities of the Authority

1. Without being restricted by financial controls, regulations or moratoriums of any kind, the Authority may freely:
(a) purchase any currencies through authorized channels and hold and dispose of them;
(b) hold funds, securities, gold, precious metals or currency of any kind and operate accounts in any currency;
(c) transfer its funds, securities, gold or currency from one country to another or within any country and convert any currency held by it into any other currency.

2. The Authority shall, in exercising its rights under paragraph 1 of this article, pay due regard to any representations made by the Government of any member of the Authority insofar as it is considered that effect can be given to such representations without detriment to the interests of the Authority.

Article 6
Flag and emblem

The Authority shall be entitled to display its flag and emblem at its premises and on vehicles used for official purposes.

Article 7
Representatives of members of the Authority

1.   Representatives of members of the Authority attending meetings convened by the Authority shall, while exercising their functions and during their journey to and from the place of meeting, enjoy the following privileges and immunities:

(a)   immunity from legal process in respect of words spoken or written, and all acts performed by them in the exercise of their functions, except to the extent that the member which they represent expressly waives this immunity in a particular case;

(b)   immunity from personal arrest or detention and the same immunities and facilities in respect of their personal baggage as are accorded to diplomatic envoys;

(c)   inviolability for all papers and documents;

(d)   the right to use codes and to receive papers or correspondence by courier or in sealed bags;

(e)   exemption in respect of themselves and their spouses from immigration restrictions, alien registration or national service obligations in the State they are visiting or through which they are passing in the exercise of their functions;

(f)   the same facilities as regards exchange restrictions as are accorded to representatives of foreign Governments of comparable rank on temporary official missions.

2.   In order to secure, for the representatives of members of the Authority, complete freedom of speech and independence in the discharge of their duties, the immunity from legal process in respect of all acts done by them in discharging their functions shall continue to be accorded, notwithstanding that the persons concerned are no longer representatives of members of the Authority.

3.   Where the incidence of any form of taxation depends upon residence, periods during which the representatives of members of the Authority attending the meetings of the Authority are present in the territory of a member of the Authority for the discharge of their duties shall not be considered as periods of residence.

4.   Privileges and immunities are accorded to the representatives of members of the Authority, not for the personal benefit of the individuals themselves, but in order to safeguard the independent exercise of their functions in connection with the Authority. Consequently, a member of the Authority has the right and the duty to waive the immunity of its representative in any case where in the opinion of the member of the Authority the immunity would impede the course of justice, and it can be waived without prejudice to the purpose for which the immunity is accorded.

5.   Representatives of members of the Authority shall have insurance coverage against third-party risks in respect of vehicles owned or operated by them, as required by the laws and regulations of the State in which the vehicle is operated.

6.   The provisions of paragraphs 1, 2 and 3 are not applicable as between a representative and the authorities of the member of the Authority of which he or she is a national or of which he or she is or has been a representative.

Article 8
Officials

1.   The Secretary-General will specify the categories of officials to which the provisions of paragraph 2 of this article shall apply. The Secretary-General shall submit these categories to the Assembly. Thereafter these categories shall be communicated to the Governments of all members of the Authority. The names of the officials included in these categories shall from time to time be made known to the Governments of members of the Authority.

2.   Officials of the Authority, regardless of nationality, shall:

(a)   be immune from legal process in respect of words spoken or written and all acts performed by them in their official capacity;

(b)   be immune from personal arrest or detention in relation to acts performed by them in their official capacity;

(c)   be exempt from tax in respect of salaries and emoluments paid or any other form of payment made by the Authority;

(d)   be immune from national service obligations provided that, in relation to States of which they are nationals, such immunity shall be confined to officials of the Authority whose names have, by reason of their duties, been placed upon a list compiled by the Secretary-General and approved by the State concerned; should other officials of the Authority be called up for national service, the State concerned shall, at the request of the Secretary-General, grant such temporary deferments in the call-up of such officials as may be necessary to avoid interruption in the continuation of essential work;

(e)   be exempt, together with their spouses and relatives dependent on them, from immigration restrictions and alien registration;

(f)   be accorded the same privileges in respect of exchange facilities as are accorded to the officials of comparable ranks forming part of diplomatic missions to the Governments concerned;

(g)   have the right to import free of duty their furniture and effects at the time of first taking up their post in the country in question;

(h)   be exempt from inspection of personal baggage, unless there are serious grounds for believing that the baggage contains articles not for personal use or articles the import or export of which is prohibited by the law or controlled by the quarantine regulations of the Party concerned; and inspection in such a case shall be conducted in the presence of the official concerned, and in the case of official baggage, in the presence of the Secretary-General or his or her authorized representative;

(i)   be given, together with their spouses and relatives dependent on them, the same repatriation facilities in time of international crises as are accorded to diplomatic agents.

3.   In addition to the privileges and immunities specified in paragraph 2, the Secretary-General or any official acting on his behalf during his absence from duty and the Director-General of the Enterprise shall be accorded in respect of themselves, their spouses and minor children the privileges and immunities, exemptions and facilities accorded to diplomatic envoys, in accordance with international law.

4.   Privileges and immunities are accorded to officials, not for the personal benefit of the individuals themselves, but in order to safeguard the independent exercise of their functions in connection with the Authority. The Secretary-General has the right and the duty to waive the immunity of any official where, in the opinion of the Secretary-General, the immunity would impede the course of justice, and it can be waived without prejudice to the interests of the Authority. In the case of the Secretary-General, the Assembly shall have the right to waive immunity.

5.   The Authority shall cooperate at all times with the appropriate authorities of members of the Authority to facilitate the proper administration of justice, secure the observance of police regulations and prevent the occurrence of any abuse in connection with the privileges, immunities and facilities referred to in this article.

6.   Pursuant to the laws and regulations of the State concerned, the officials of the Authority shall be required to have insurance coverage against third-party risks in respect of vehicles owned or operated by them.

Article 9
Experts on mission for the Authority

1.   Experts (other than officials coming within the scope of article 8) performing missions for the Authority shall be accorded such privileges and immunities as are necessary for the independent exercise of their functions during the period of their missions, including the time spent on journeys in connection with their missions. In particular they shall be accorded:

(a)   immunity from personal arrest or detention and from seizure of their personal baggage;

(b)   in respect of words spoken or written and acts done by them in the exercise of their functions, immunity from legal process of every kind. This immunity shall continue notwithstanding that the persons concerned are no longer employed on missions for the Authority;

(c)   inviolability for all papers and documents;

(d)   for the purposes of their communications with the Authority, the right to use codes and to receive papers or correspondence by courier or in sealed bags;

(e)   exemption from tax in respect of salaries and emoluments paid or any other form of payment made by the Authority. This provision is not applicable as between an expert and the member of the Authority of which he or she is a national;

(f)   the same facilities in respect of currency or exchange restrictions as are accorded to representatives of foreign Governments on temporary official missions.

2.   Privileges and immunities are accorded to experts, not for the personal benefit of the individuals themselves, but in order to safeguard the independent exercise of their functions in connection with the Authority. The Secretary-General shall have the right and the duty to waive the immunity of any expert where, in the opinion of the Secretary-General, the immunity would impede the course of justice, and it can be waived without prejudice to the interests of the Authority.

Article 10
Respect for laws and regulations

Without prejudice to their privileges and immunities, it is the duty of all persons referred to in articles 7, 8 and 9 to respect the laws and regulations of the member of the Authority in whose territory they may be on the business of the Authority or through whose territory they may pass on such business. They also have a duty not to interfere in the internal affairs of that member.

Article 11
Laissez-passer and visas

1.   Without prejudice to the possibility for the Authority to issue its own travel documents, the States Parties to this Protocol shall recognize and accept the United Nations laissez-passer issued to officials of the Authority.

2.   Applications for visas (where required) from officials of the Authority shall be dealt with as speedily as possible. Applications for visas (where required) from officials of the Authority holding United Nations laissez-passer shall be accompanied by a document confirming that they are travelling on the official business of the Authority.

Article 12
Relationship between the Headquarters Agreement and the Protocol

The provisions of this Protocol shall be complementary to the provisions of the Headquarters Agreement. Insofar as any provision of this Protocol relates to the same subject matter, the two provisions shall, wherever possible, be treated as complementary, so that both provisions shall be applicable and neither shall narrow the effect of the other; but in any case of conflict, the provisions of that Agreement shall prevail.

Article 13
Supplementary agreements

This Protocol shall in no way limit or prejudice the privileges and immunities which have been, or may hereafter be, accorded to the Authority by any member of the Authority by reason of the location in the territory of that member of the Authority's headquarters or regional centres or offices. This Protocol shall not be deemed to prevent the conclusion of supplementary agreements between the Authority and any member of the Authority.

Article 14
Settlement of disputes

1.   In connection with the implementation of the privileges and immunities granted under this Protocol, the Authority shall make suitable provision for the proper settlement of:
  (a) disputes of a private law character to which the Authority is a party;
  (b) disputes involving any official of the Authority or any expert on mission for the Authority who by reason of his or her official position enjoys immunity, if immunity has not been waived by the Secretary-General.

2.   Any dispute between the Authority and a member of the Authority concerning the interpretation or application of this Protocol which is not settled by consultation, negotiation or other agreed mode of settlement within three months following a request by one of the parties to the dispute shall, at the request of either party, be referred for a final and binding decision to a panel of three arbitrators:
  (a) one to be nominated by the Secretary-General, one to be nominated by the other party to the dispute and the third, who shall be Chairman of the panel, to be chosen by the first two arbitrators;
  (b) if either party has failed to make its appointment of an arbitrator within two months of the appointment of an arbitrator by the other party, the President of the International Tribunal for the Law of the Sea shall proceed to make such appointment. Should the first two arbitrators fail to agree upon the appointment of the third arbitrator within three months following the appointment of the first two arbitrators, the third arbitrator shall be chosen by the President of the International Tribunal for the Law of the Sea upon the request of the Secretary-General or the other party to the dispute.

Article 15
Signature

This Protocol shall be open for signature by all members of the Authority at the headquarters of the International Seabed Authority in Kingston, Jamaica, from 17 August until 28 August 1998 and subsequently until 16 August 2000 at United Nations Headquarters in New York.

Article 16
Ratification

This Protocol is subject to ratification, approval or acceptance. The instruments of ratification, approval or acceptance shall be deposited with the Secretary-General of the United Nations.

Article 17
Accession

This Protocol shall remain open for accession by all members of the Authority at any time. The instruments of accession shall be deposited with the Secretary-General of the United Nations.

Article 18
Entry into force

1.   The Protocol shall enter into force 30 days after the date of deposit of the tenth instrument of ratification, approval, acceptance or accession.

2.   For each member of the Authority which ratifies, approves or accepts this Protocol or accedes thereto after the deposit of the tenth instrument of ratification, approval, acceptance or accession, this Protocol shall enter into force on the thirtieth day following the deposit of its instrument of ratification, approval, acceptance or accession.

Article 19
Provisional application

A State which intends to ratify, approve, accept or accede to this Protocol may at any time notify the depositary that it will apply this Protocol provisionally for a period not exceeding two years.

Article 20
Denunciation

1.   A State Party may, by written notification addressed to the Secretary-General of the United Nations, denounce this Protocol. The denunciation shall take effect one year after the date of receipt of the notification, unless the notification specifies a later date.

2.   The denunciation shall not in any way affect the duty of any State Party to fulfil any obligation embodied in this Protocol to which it would be subject under international law independently of this Protocol.

Article 21
Depositary

The Secretary-General of the United Nations shall be the depositary of this Protocol.

Article 22
Authentic texts

The Arabic, Chinese, English, French, Russian and Spanish texts of this Protocol are equally authentic.

IN WITNESS WHEREOF, the undersigned Plenipotentiaries, being duly authorized thereto, have signed the Protocol.

OPENED FOR SIGNATURE at Kingston, the twenty-sixth day of August one thousand nine hundred and ninety-eight, in a single original, in the Arabic, Chinese, English, French, Russian and Spanish languages.

COMMENTARY

Section 4, subsection G of the 1982 Convention deals with the legal status, privileges, and immunities of the International Seabed Authority and of certain persons connected with the Authority. It was modelled on other instruments, including articles 104 and 105 of the Charter of the United Nations, the Convention on the Privileges and Immunities of the United Nations of 13 February 1946, and the Convention on the Privileges and Immunities of the Specialized Agencies of 21 November 1947.

On the basis of these provisions, the Preparatory Commission elaborated and presented to the Authority, at the first session of the Assembly in August 1995, a Final Draft Protocol on the Privileges and Immunities of the International Seabed Authority. Toward the end of its first session, the Assembly of the Authority set up an ad hoc working group, chaired by Mr. Marsit (Tunisia), to review this final draft.

During the resumed second session of the Assembly, held from 5 to 16 August 1996, the working group was reconvened and held six further meetings under the chairmanship of Mr. Zdislaw Galicki (Poland). It continued to meet during the third session of the Assembly (1997) under the same chairmanship. Discussions in the working group were centred on the fact that some members of the Authority preferred a detailed protocol similar to that proposed by the Preparatory Commission, while others argued for a short document containing only those essential matters not covered in the 1982 Convention. Some States preferred to dispense with a protocol altogether, simply relying upon the provisions of the 1982 Convention as the sole basis for the privileges and immunities of the Authority.

At the end of the resumed third session of the Authority in August 1997, the working group had produced a revised draft of the Protocol in the form of an informal working paper for submission to the Assembly. The final draft Protocol was a much-shortened version of the draft proposed by the Preparatory Commission. It deals with the immunities and privileges of the Authority in relation to those matters which are not already covered in the 1982 Convention and is based substantially on articles I, II, IV, V, VI and VII of the Convention on the Privileges and Immunities of the United Nations (1946) as well as the Convention on the Privileges and Immunities of the Specialized Agencies (1947). These include immunities and privileges of representatives travelling to and from the seat of the Authority and the use of the United Nations *laissez-passer* by staff of the Authority. The protocol also elaborates upon the privileges and immunities to be accorded to certain categories of persons, including officials of the Authority, experts on mission, and representatives of members of the Authority.

At its fifty-fourth meeting, on 26 March 1998, the Assembly adopted by consensus the Protocol on the Privileges and Immunities of the International Seabed Authority, as proposed by the working group. In order to facilitate signature of the Protocol by member States, the Protocol was opened for signature at the headquarters of the Authority at a formal ceremony on 26-27 August 1998 and subsequently until 16 August 2000 at United Nations Headquarters in New York. The following members of the Authority signed the Protocol in Kingston: Bahamas, Brazil, Indonesia, Jamaica, Kenya, the Netherlands and Trinidad and Tobago. The following signed during the time the Protocol was open for signature at UN Headquarters: Chile, Côte d'Ivoire, Czech Republic, Egypt, Finland, Ghana, Greece, Italy, Malta, Namibia, Oman, Pakistan, Portugal, Saudi Arabia, Senegal, Slovakia, Spain, Sudan, The former Yugoslav Republic of Macedonia, the United Kingdom of Great Britain and Northern Ireland and Uruguay.

On 1 May 2003, Nigeria became the tenth member of the Authority to ratify, accept or accede to the Protocol. In accordance with its article 18, paragraph 1, the Protocol therefore entered into force on 31 May 2003. As at 4 October 2012, the following 36 members of the Authority are parties to the Protocol on the Privileges and Immunities of the International Seabed Authority: Argentina, Austria, Brazil, Bulgaria, Cameroon, Chile, Croatia, Cuba, Czech Republic, Denmark, Egypt, Estonia, Finland, France, Germany, Guyana, India, Ireland, Italy, Jamaica, Lithuania, Mauritius, Mozambique, Netherlands, Nigeria, Norway, Oman, Poland, Portugal, Slovakia, Slovenia, Spain, Togo, Trinidad and Tobago, United Kingdom of Great Britain and Northern Ireland and Uruguay.

DOCUMENTARY SOURCES

- PREPARATORY COMMISSION
LOS/PCN/WP.49/Rev.2, Final draft Protocol on the Privileges and Immunities of the International Seabed Authority, reproduced in: LOS/PCN/153, Vol. V, p.126-141.
- ISBA
ISBA/3/A/L.4, Statement of the President on the work of the Assembly during the third session, paras. 5-8, (*Selected Decisions 1/2/3*, 44).
ISBA/3/A/4, Report of the Secretary-General of the International Seabed Authority under article 166, paragraph 4, of the United Nations Convention on the Law of the Sea, para. 13, (*Selected Decisions 1/2/3*, 48).

ISBA/3/A/11, Statement of the President on the work of the Assembly during the resumed third session, paras. 2-4, (*Selected Decisions 1/2/3*, 61-62).

ISBA/3/A/WP.1, Draft protocol on the Privileges and Immunities of the Authority. Prepared by the Secretariat.

ISBA/3/A/WP.1/Add.1, Revised draft protocol on the Privileges and Immunities of the Authority. Prepared by the Secretariat.

ISBA/4/A/8, Decision of the Assembly of the International Seabed Authority relating to the Protocol on the Privileges and Immunities of the International Seabed Authority, (*Selected Decisions 4*, 42-49).

ISBA/4/A/9, Statement of the President on the work of the Assembly during the fourth session, paras. 10-13, (*Selected Decisions 4*, 51).

ISBA/4/A/11, Report of the Secretary-General of the International Seabed Authority under article 166, paragraph 4, of the United Nations Convention on the Law of the Sea, paras. 21-22, (*Selected Decisions 4*, 55-56).

ISBA/4/A/18, Statement of the President on the work of the Assembly during the resumed fourth session, para. 10, (*Selected Decisions 4*, 65).

ISBA/4/A/L.2, Draft protocol on the Privileges and Immunities of the International Seabed Authority.

ISBA/5/A/1 and Corr. 1, Report of the Secretary-General of the International Seabed Authority under article 166, paragraph 4, of the United Nations Convention on the Law of Sea, para. 9, (*Selected Decisions 5*, 2).

ISBA/6/A/9, Report of the Secretary-General of the International Seabed Authority under article 166, paragraph 4, of the United Nations Convention on the Law of the Sea, para. 11, (*Selected Decisions 6*, 14).

ISBA/7/A/2, Report of the Secretary-General of the International Seabed Authority under article 166, paragraph 4, of the United Nations Convention on the Law of the Sea, para. 11, (*Selected Decisions 7*, 6).

ISBA/7/A/7, Statement of the President on the work of the Assembly at the seventh session, para. 10, (*Selected Decisions 7*, 18).

ISBA/8/A/5, Report of the Secretary-General of the International Seabed Authority under article 166, paragraph 4, of the United Nations Convention on the Law of the Sea, para. 9, (*Selected Decisions 8*, 10-11).

ISBA/8/A/13, Statement of the President on the work of the Assembly at the eighth session, para. 8, (*Selected Decisions 8*, 32).

STATUS OF THE PROTOCOL ON THE PRIVILEGES AND IMMUNITIES OF THE INTERNATIONAL SEABED AUTHORITY (AS AT 4 OCTOBER 2012)

	States	*Signature*	*Ratification, Approval (AA), Acceptance (A), or Accession (a)*
21	Argentina		20 October 2006 (a)
11	Austria		25 September 2003 (a)
	Bahamas	26 August 1998	
26	Brazil	27 August 1998	16 November 2007
31	Bulgaria		10 February 2009 (a)
7	Cameroon		28 August 2002 (a)
15	Chile	14 April 1999	8 February 2005
	Côte d'Ivoire	25 September 1998	
2	Croatia		8 September 2000 (a)
29	Cuba		11 July 2008 (a)
6	Czech Republic	1 August 2000	26 October 2001
13	Denmark		16 November 2004 (a)
5	Egypt	26 April 2000	20 June 2001
27	Estonia		1 February 2008 (a)
25	Finland	31 March 1999	31 October 2007 (A)
34	France		23 January 2012 (a)
23	Germany		8 June 2007 (a)
	Ghana	12 January 1999	
	Greece	14 October 1998	
33	Guyana		25 October 2011 (a)
17	India		14 November 2005 (a)
	Indonesia	26 August 1998	
32	Ireland		9 February 2011 (a)
20	Italy	18 May 2000	19 July 2006
8	Jamaica	26 August 1998	25 September 2002
	Kenya	26 August 1998	
36	Lithuania		26 September 2012 (a)
	Malta	26 July 2000	

14	Mauritius		22 December 2004 (a)
30	Mozambique		12 January 2009 (a)
	Namibia	24 September 1999	
9	Netherlands	26 August 1998	21 November 2002 (A)
10	Nigeria		1 May 2003 (a)
18	Norway		10 May 2006 (a)
12	Oman	19 August 1999	12 March 2004
	Pakistan	9 September 1999	
24	Poland		2 October 2007 (a)
22	Portugal	6 April 2000	2 February 2007
	Saudi Arabia	11 October 1999	
	Senegal	11 June 1999	
1	Slovakia	22 June 1999	20 April 2000
28	Slovenia		1 April 2008 (a)
4	Spain	14 September 1999	9 January 2001
	Sudan	6 August 1999	
	The Former Yugoslav Republic of Macedonia	17 September 1998	
35	Togo		11 June 2012 (a)
16	Trinidad and Tobago	26 August 1998	10 August 2005
3	United Kingdom of Great Britain and Northern Ireland	19 August 1999	2 November 2000
19	Uruguay	21 October 1998	6 July 2006 (a)

DECLARATIONS AND RESERVATIONS

(Unless otherwise indicated, the declarations and reservations were made upon ratification, approval, acceptance or accession.)

Argentina

Declaration:
The Republic of Argentina will accord such privileges and immunities as are specified in the Protocol on the Privileges and Immunities of the International

Seabed Authority, adopted in Kingston on 27 March 1998, to members of the Secretariat of the International Seabed Authority who are nationals or permanent residents in its territory to the extent necessary for the adequate fulfillment of their duties. With regard to fiscal and customs matters those members will be subject to the national norms applied in its territory.

Chile

Reservation:

The Government of Chile expresses a reservation with respect to article 8, paragraph 2 (d) of the Protocol, as that provision will not exempt its nationals from national service obligations.

Cuba

Declaration:

Article 14, paragraph 2 (a) and (b), of the Protocol shall not apply to the Republic of Cuba, which shall settle on a bilateral basis, by negotiation, any dispute arising with the International Seabed Authority concerning the interpretation or application of the aforementioned Protocol.

France

Reservation:

France intends to limit the exemption from taxation provided for in articles 8 (c) and 9 (e) of the Protocol:

- To the officials of the Authority referred to in article 8, excluding the experts on mission for the Authority referred to in article 9;

- To the salaries and emoluments received from the Authority by these officials, excluding any other form of payment which may be made to them by the Authority.

TERRITORIAL APPLICATION

States	Date of receipt of the notification	Territories
Netherlands	7 January 2009	Netherlands Antilles

II – EXTERNAL RELATIONS OF THE INTERNATIONAL SEABED AUTHORITY

According to article 169 of the 1982 Convention, the Secretary-General of the International Seabed Authority shall, on matters within the competence of the International Seabed Authority, make suitable arrangements, with the approval of the Council pursuant to article 162, paragraph 2 (f), for consultation and co-operation with international and non-governmental organizations recognized by the Economic and Social Council of the United Nations.

The relationship established through arrangements entered into pursuant to article 169 is to be distinguished from observer status granted in accordance with the rules of procedure of the organs of the Authority. Under its rules of procedure, the Assembly has granted observer status to a number of intergovernmental and non-governmental organizations, notwithstanding the fact that no cooperative arrangements between the Authority and such organizations have been established pursuant to article 169. This may be contrasted with the situation in the General Assembly of the United Nations where consultative status with the Economic and Social Council remains at the core of the formal relationship between the United Nations and non-governmental organizations.

A – RELATIONS WITH INTERNATIONAL ORGANIZATIONS

RELATIONS WITH THE UNITED NATIONS

DECISION OF THE ASSEMBLY CONCERNING THE OBSERVER STATUS OF THE INTERNATIONAL SEABED AUTHORITY AT THE UNITED NATIONS

The Assembly of the International Seabed Authority,

Noting that the United Nations General Assembly by its resolutions 49/28 and 50/23 dated 6 December 1994 and 5 December 1995, respectively, emphasized that activities governed by the United Nations Convention on the Law of the Sea are closely interrelated and need to be considered as a whole, and therefore reaffirmed the importance of the annual consideration and review by the General Assembly of overall developments pertaining to the implementation of the Convention as well as of other developments relating to the law of the sea and ocean affairs,

Bearing in mind that the International Seabed Authority, as an autonomous international organization under the Convention, is the organization through which States parties to the Convention shall, in accordance with the regime for the Area established in Part XI and the Implementing Agreement, organize and control activities in the Area, particularly with a view to administering resources of the Area,

Recognizing that the Authority, due to its responsibilities under the Convention, has an interest in matters relating to the law of the sea and ocean affairs annually considered by the General Assembly of the United Nations,

1. *Decides* that the International Seabed Authority should seek to obtain observer status at the United Nations to enable it to participate in the deliberations of the General Assembly;

2. *Requests* the Secretary-General of the International Seabed Authority to take the necessary measures to seek such observer status.

39th meeting
26 August 1996

RESOLUTION ADOPTED BY THE GENERAL ASSEMBLY

[without reference to a Main Committee (A/51/L.2 and Add.1)]

51/6. OBSERVER STATUS FOR THE INTERNATIONAL SEABED AUTHORITY IN THE GENERAL ASSEMBLY

The General Assembly,

Aware of the importance of the effective implementation of the United Nations Convention on the Law of the Sea of 10 December 1982[1] and of the Agreement relating to the Implementation of Part XI of the United Nations Convention on the Law of the Sea,[2] and their uniform consistent application, as well as of the growing need to promote and facilitate international cooperation on the law of the sea and ocean affairs at the global, regional and subregional levels,

Noting the decision of the Assembly of the International Seabed Authority at its resumed second session to seek observer status for the Authority at the United Nations in order to enable it to participate in the deliberations of the General Assembly,

1.   *Decides* to invite the International Seabed Authority to participate in the deliberations of the General Assembly in the capacity of observer;

2.   *Requests* the Secretary-General to take the necessary action to implement the present resolution.

40th plenary meeting
24 October 1996

COMMENTARY

Bearing in mind the particular status of the Authority as an autonomous international organization under the 1982 Convention, the Assembly, at its resumed second session in August 1996, requested the Secretary-General to seek on behalf of the Authority observer status at the United Nations in order to enable the Authority to participate in the deliberations of the General Assembly (ISBA/A/13 and Corr. 1). On 24 October 1996, by General Assembly resolution 51/6, the Authority was granted observer status (A/RES/51/6). Such participation is particularly appropriate given the General Assembly's annual debate on Oceans and the Law of the Sea, and its overall coordinating role in this field.

---

[1]   *Official Records of the Third United Nations Conference on the Law of the Sea*, vol. XVII (United Nations publication, Sales No. E.84.V.3), document A/CONF.62/122.
[2]   Resolution 48/263, annex.

Likewise, the General Assembly of the United Nations, at its fifty-first session, granted observer status to the International Tribunal of the Law of the Sea (A/RES/51/204) on 17 December 1996.

DOCUMENTARY SOURCES

- ISBA

ISBA/A/13 and Corr. 1, Decision of the Assembly concerning the observer status of the International Seabed Authority at the United Nations, (*Selected Decisions 1/2/3*, 26).

ISBA/A/L.13, Statement of the President on the work of the Assembly during the resumed second session, para. 19, (*Selected Decisions 1/2/3*, 32).

ISBA/3/A/4, Report of the Secretary-General of the International Seabed Authority under article 166, paragraph 4, of the United Nations Convention on the Law of the Sea, para. 19, (*Selected Decisions 1/2/3*, 49-50).

- UNITED NATIONS

A/RES/51/6, Observer status for the International Seabed Authority in the General Assembly.

AGREEMENT CONCERNING THE RELATIONSHIP BETWEEN THE UNITED NATIONS AND THE INTERNATIONAL SEABED AUTHORITY

The United Nations and the International Seabed Authority,

Bearing in mind that the General Assembly of the United Nations in its resolution 3067 (XXVIII) of 16 November 1973 decided to convene the Third United Nations Conference on the Law of the Sea for the adoption of a convention dealing with all matters relating to the law of the sea and that the Conference adopted the United Nations Convention on the Law of the Sea, which, *inter alia,* establishes the International Seabed Authority,

Recalling that the General Assembly of the United Nations in its resolution 48/263 of 28 July 1994 adopted the Agreement relating to the Implementation of Part XI of the United Nations Convention on the Law of the Sea of 10 December 1982,

Mindful of the entry into force of the United Nations Convention on the Law of the Sea on 16 November 1994 and the entry into force of the Agreement relating to the Implementation of Part XI of the United Nations Convention on the Law of the Sea of 10 December 1982 on 28 July 1996,

Noting General Assembly resolution 51/6 of 24 October 1996 inviting the International Seabed Authority to participate in the deliberations of the General Assembly in the capacity of observer,

Noting further article 162, paragraph 2 (f), of the United Nations Convention on the Law of the Sea of 10 December 1982, General Assembly resolution 51/34 of 9 December 1996 and decision ISBA/C/10 of 12 August 1996 of the Council of the International Seabed Authority calling for the conclusion of a relationship agreement between the United Nations and the International Seabed Authority,

Desiring to make provision for an effective system of mutually beneficial relationship whereby the discharge of their respective responsibilities may be facilitated,

Taking into account for this purpose the provisions of the Charter of the United Nations, the provisions of the United Nations Convention on the Law of the Sea and the provisions of the Agreement relating to the Implementation of Part XI of the United Nations Convention on the Law of the Sea of 10 December 1982,

Have agreed as follows:

Article 1
Purpose of the Agreement

This Agreement, which is entered into by the United Nations and the International Seabed Authority (hereinafter referred to as "the Authority"), pursuant to the provisions of the Charter of the United Nations (hereinafter referred to as "the Charter") and the provisions of the United Nations Convention on the Law of the Sea (hereinafter referred to as "the Convention") and the Agreement relating to the Implementation of Part XI of the United Nations Convention on the Law of the Sea of 10 December 1982 (hereinafter referred to as "the Agreement") respectively, is intended to define the terms on which the United Nations and the Authority shall be brought into relationship.

Article 2
Principles

1. The United Nations recognizes the Authority as the organization through which States Parties to the Convention shall, in accordance with Part XI of the Convention and the Agreement, organize and control activities in the seabed and ocean floor and subsoil thereof, beyond the limits of national jurisdiction (hereinafter referred to as "the Area"), particularly with a view to administering the resources of the Area. The United Nations undertakes to conduct its activities in such a manner as to promote the legal order for the seas and oceans established by the Convention and the Agreement.

2. The United Nations recognizes that the Authority, by virtue of the Convention and the Agreement, shall function as an autonomous international organization in the working relationship with the United Nations established by this Agreement.

3. The Authority recognizes the responsibilities of the United Nations under the Charter and other international instruments, in particular in the fields of international peace and security and economic, social, cultural and humanitarian development, protection and preservation of the environment.

4. The Authority undertakes to conduct its activities in accordance with the purposes and principles of the Charter to promote peace and international cooperation and in conformity with the policies of the United Nations furthering these purposes and principles.

Article 3
Cooperation and coordination

1. The United Nations and the Authority recognize the desirability of achieving effective coordination of the activities of the Authority with those of the United Nations and the specialized agencies, and of avoiding unnecessary duplication of activities.

2. The United Nations and the Authority agree that, with a view to facilitating the effective discharge of their respective responsibilities, they will cooperate closely with each other and consult each other on matters of mutual interest.

Article 4
Assistance to the Security Council

1.   The Authority shall cooperate with the Security Council by providing to it at its request such information and assistance as may be required in the exercise of its responsibility for the maintenance or restoration of international peace and security. In case confidential information is provided, the Security Council shall preserve its confidential character.

2.   At the invitation of the Security Council, the Secretary-General of the Authority may attend its meetings to supply it with information or give it other assistance with regard to matters within the competence of the Authority.

Article 5
International Court of Justice

The Authority agrees, subject to the provisions of this Agreement relating to the safeguarding of confidential material, data and information, to provide any information which may be requested by the International Court of Justice in accordance with the Statute of that Court.

Article 6
Reciprocal representation

1.   Without prejudice to the decision of the General Assembly in resolution 51/6 of 24 October 1996 granting observer status to the Authority, and subject to such decisions as may be taken concerning the attendance of their meetings by observers, the United Nations shall, subject to the rules of procedure and practice of the bodies concerned, invite the Authority to send representatives to meetings and conferences of other competent bodies, whenever matters of interest to the Authority are discussed.

2.   Subject to such decisions as may be taken by its competent bodies concerning the attendance of their meetings by observers, the Authority shall, subject to the rules of procedure and practice of the bodies concerned, invite the United Nations to send representatives to all its meetings and conferences, whenever matters of interest to the United Nations are discussed.

3.   Written statements submitted by the United Nations to the Authority for distribution shall be distributed by the secretariat of the Authority to all members of the appropriate organ or organs of the Authority in accordance with the relevant rules of procedure. Written statements presented by the Authority to the United Nations for distribution shall be distributed by the Secretariat of the United Nations to all members of the appropriate organ or organs of the United Nations in accordance with the relevant rules of procedure. Such written statements will be circulated in the quantities and languages in which they are made available to the respective secretariat.

Article 7
Cooperation between the two secretariats

The Secretary-General of the United Nations and the Secretary-General of the Authority shall consult from time to time regarding the implementation of their respective responsibilities under the Convention and the Agreement. They shall consult, in particular, regarding such administrative arrangements as may be necessary to enable the two organizations effectively to carry out their functions and to ensure effective cooperation and liaison between their secretariats.

Article 8
Exchange of information, data and documents

1.   The United Nations and the Authority shall arrange for the exchange of information, publications and reports of mutual interest.

2.   In fulfilment of the responsibilities entrusted to him under article 319, subparagraphs 2 (a) and (b) of the Convention and assumed by him pursuant to General Assembly resolution 37/66 of 3 December 1982, the Secretary-General of the United Nations shall report to the Authority from time to time on issues of a general nature that have arisen with respect to the Convention and shall regularly notify the Authority of ratifications and formal confirmations of and accessions to the Convention and amendments thereto, as well as of denunciations of the Convention.

3.   The United Nations and the Authority shall cooperate in obtaining from States Parties to the Convention copies of charts or lists of geographical coordinates of the outer limit lines of their continental shelf as referred to in article 84 of the Convention. They will exchange copies of such lists of coordinates or, to the extent practicable, charts.

4.   Where the outer limits of the national jurisdiction of a State Party are defined by the outer limit of the exclusive economic zone, the United Nations shall provide to the Authority copies of such lists of geographical coordinates or, to the extent practicable, charts, indicating the outer limit lines of the exclusive economic zone of such State Party as may be deposited with the Secretary-General of the United Nations pursuant to article 75, paragraph 2 of the Convention.

5.   The Authority, to the extent practicable, shall furnish special studies or information requested by the United Nations. The submission of such reports, studies and information shall be subject to conditions set forth in article 14.

6.   The United Nations and the Authority are subject to necessary limitations for the safeguarding of confidential material, data and information furnished to them by their members or others. Subject to article 4, paragraph 1, nothing in this Agreement shall be construed to require either the United Nations or the Authority to furnish any material, data and information the furnishing of which could, in its judgement, constitute a violation of the confidence of any of its members or anyone from whom it shall have received such information, or which would otherwise interfere with the orderly conduct of its operation.

Article 9
Statistical services

The United Nations and the Authority, recognizing the desirability of maximum cooperation in the statistical field and of minimizing the burdens placed on Governments and other organizations from which information may be collected, undertake to avoid undesirable duplication between them with respect to the collection, analysis and publication of statistics, and agree to consult with each other on the most efficient use of resources and of technical personnel in the field of statistics.

Article 10
Technical assistance

The United Nations and the Authority undertake to work together in the provision of technical assistance in the fields of marine scientific research in the Area, transfer of technology and the prevention, reduction and control of pollution of the marine environment from activities in the Area. In particular, they agree to take such measures as may be necessary to achieve effective coordination of their technical assistance activities within the framework of existing coordinating machinery in the field of technical assistance, taking into account the respective roles and responsibilities of the United Nations and the Authority under their constitutive instruments, as well as those of other organizations participating in technical assistance activities.

Article 11
Personnel arrangements

1.   The United Nations and the Authority agree to apply, in the interests of uniform standards of international employment and to the extent feasible, common personnel standards, methods and arrangements designed to avoid unjustified differences in terms and conditions of employment and to facilitate interchange of personnel in order to obtain the maximum benefit from their services.

2.   To this end, the United Nations and the Authority agree:

(a) To consult together from time to time concerning matters of common interest relating to the terms and conditions of employment of the officers and staff, with a view to securing as much uniformity in these matters as may be feasible;

(b) To cooperate in the interchange of personnel when desirable, on a temporary or a permanent basis, making due provision for the retention of seniority and pension rights;

(c) To cooperate in the establishment and operation of suitable machinery for the settlement of disputes arising in connection with the employment of personnel and related matters.

3.   Pursuant to decision ISBA/A/15 of 15 August 1996 of the Assembly of the International Seabed Authority, and upon the approval of the General Assembly

of the United Nations, the Authority shall participate in the United Nations Joint Staff Pension Fund in accordance with the Regulations of the Fund and shall accept the jurisdiction of the United Nations Administrative Tribunal in matters involving applications alleging non-observance of those Regulations.

4.   The terms and conditions on which any facilities or services of the Authority or the United Nations in connection with the matters referred to in this article are to be extended to the other shall, where necessary, be the subject of supplementary arrangements concluded for this purpose.

Article 12
Conference services

1.   Unless the General Assembly of the United Nations, after giving reasonable notice to the Authority, decides otherwise, the United Nations will make available to the Authority, on a reimbursable basis, such facilities and services as may be required for the meetings of the Authority, including translation and interpretation services, documentation and conference services.

2.   The terms and conditions on which any facilities or services of the United Nations in connection with the matters referred to in this article may be extended to the Authority shall, where necessary, be the subject of separate agreements concluded for this purpose.

Article 13
Budgetary and financial matters

The Authority recognizes the desirability of establishing close budgetary and financial cooperation with the United Nations aimed at benefiting from the experience of the United Nations in this field.

Article 14
Financing of services

The costs and expenses resulting from the provision of services pursuant to this Agreement shall be the subject of separate arrangements between the Authority and the United Nations.

Article 15
United Nations laissez-passer

Without prejudice to the right of the Authority to issue its own travel documents, officials of the Authority shall be entitled, in accordance with such special arrangements as may be concluded between the Secretary-General of the United Nations and the Secretary-General of the Authority, to use the laissez-passer of the United Nations as a valid travel document where such use is recognized under the Protocol on the Privileges and Immunities of the International Seabed Authority or other agreements defining the privileges and immunities of the Authority.

Article 16
Implementation of the Agreement

The Secretary-General of the United Nations and the Secretary-General of the Authority may enter into such supplementary arrangements for the implementation of this Agreement as may be found desirable.

Article 17
Amendments

This Agreement may be amended by agreement between the United Nations and the Authority. Any such amendment agreed upon shall enter into force on its approval by the General Assembly of the United Nations and the Assembly of the Authority.

Article 18
Entry into force

1.   This Agreement shall enter into force on its approval by the General Assembly of the United Nations and the Assembly of the Authority.

2.   This Agreement shall be applied provisionally by the United Nations and the Authority upon signature by the Secretary-General of the United Nations and the Secretary-General of the Authority.

DECISION OF THE ASSEMBLY RELATING TO THE AGREEMENT CONCERNING THE RELATIONSHIP BETWEEN THE UNITED NATIONS AND THE INTERNATIONAL SEABED AUTHORITY

The Assembly of the International Seabed Authority,

Acting on the recommendation of the Council,[1]

Having examined, at its forty-fifth meeting on 27 March 1997, the Agreement concerning the relationship between the United Nations and the International Seabed Authority,[2]

Approves the Agreement.

45th meeting
27 March 1997

---

[1] ISBA/3/C/4.
[2] ISBA/3/A/L.2.

RESOLUTION ADOPTED BY THE GENERAL ASSEMBLY

[*without reference to a Main Committee (A/52/L.27 and Add.1)*]

52/27. AGREEMENT CONCERNING THE RELATIONSHIP BETWEEN THE UNITED NATIONS AND THE INTERNATIONAL SEABED AUTHORITY

The General Assembly,

Recalling its resolution 51/34 of 9 December 1996, in which, *inter alia*, it invited the Secretary-General to take steps to conclude a relationship agreement with the International Seabed Authority, to be applied provisionally pending its approval by the General Assembly and the Assembly of the Authority,

Noting the decision of the Assembly of the International Seabed Authority at its third session[1] to approve the Agreement concerning the Relationship between the United Nations and the International Seabed Authority signed on 14 March 1997 by the Secretary-General of the United Nations and the Secretary-General of the International Seabed Authority,

Having considered the Agreement concerning the Relationship between the United Nations and the International Seabed Authority,[2]

Approves the Agreement, which is annexed to the present resolution.

57th plenary meeting
26 November 1997

(Annex not reproduced)

---

[1] ISBA/3/A/3.

[2] A/52/260, annex.

COMMENTARY

At the second session of the Authority in 1996, the Council requested the Secretary-General to negotiate with the Secretary-General of the United Nations a relationship agreement between the Authority and the United Nations taking into account the draft of such an agreement prepared by the Preparatory Commission contained in document LOS/PCN/WP.50/Rev.3. A parallel request was made by the General Assembly in the same year (A/RES/51/34). Negotiations on such an agreement took place in January 1997. The relationship agreement was negotiated and signed by the Secretary-General of the United Nations and the Secretary-General of the International Seabed Authority on 14 March 1997 in New York. According to its terms, the agreement is to be applied provisionally by the United Nations and the Authority upon signature by the respective Secretaries-General and will enter into force on its approval by the General Assembly of the United Nations and the Assembly of the Authority. At its twelfth meeting, on 20 March 1997, the agreement was approved by the Council, noting both its signature and its provisional application upon signature and recommending the Assembly to approve it. On the recommendation of the Council (contained in document ISBA/3/C/4), the relationship agreement was approved by the Assembly of the Authority at its forty-fifth meeting, on 27 March 1997 (ISBA/3/A/3 and ISBA/3/A/L.4, para. 10). It was approved by the fifty-second session of the General Assembly of the United Nations at its fifty-seventh plenary meeting in its resolution 52/27 of 26 November 1997 and entered into force on that date.

The relationship agreement establishes a mechanism for close cooperation between the secretariats of the two organizations in order to ensure effective coordination of activities and avoid unnecessary duplication of work. Such cooperative arrangements are to include cooperation regarding personnel arrangements.

Article 11 (3) of the relationship agreement refers to the participation of the Authority in the United Nations Joint Staff Pension Fund ("UNJSPF") and to the acceptation of the jurisdiction of the United Nations Administrative Tribunal in matters involving the allegations of the non-observance of the Regulations of the UNJSPF. This required the completion of several administrative steps. At its second session in August 1996, the Assembly had decided, noting the recommendation of the Preparatory Commission, that it would be in the best interest of the Authority to become a member of the UNJSPF and requested the Secretary-General to take action for that purpose. At its one hundred and eightieth meeting in July 1997, the Standing Committee of the Board of the UNJSPF, on behalf of the Board, decided to recommend to the General Assembly of the United Nations that the Authority be admitted to membership in the Fund. In decision 52/458 of 22 December 1997, the General Assembly decided to admit the Authority to membership in the Fund, with effect from 1 January 1998. In accordance with the regulations of the UNJSPF, the Secretary-General, on 18 June 1998, executed an agreement between the Fund and the Authority governing the admission of the Authority to membership. On the same date, the Authority and the United Nations also executed a special agreement extending the jurisdiction of the Administrative Tribunal of the United Nations to the Authority with respect to applications by staff members of the Authority alleging non-observance of the regulations of the UNFJSPF.

In order to give effect to article 11 (2) (c) of the relationship agreement, the United Nations and the Authority on 13 March 2003 concluded an agreement by means of an exchange of letters extending the competence of the United Nations Administrative Tribunal ("UNAT") as the appellate body to settle disputes relating to the employment of personnel of the Authority and related matters. The abolition, with effect from 31 December 2009, of the UNAT as part of the reform of the administration of justice in the United Nations, made it necessary for the United Nations and the Authority to conclude a new agreement recognizing the jurisdiction of the United Nations Appeals Tribunal to the Authority in respect of the same matters. The text of that agreement is contained in annex I to the document ISBA/16/C/4.

As envisaged in article 11 (2) (b) of the relationship Agreement, on 26 February 2001, the Authority became a party to the Inter-Organization Agreement concerning Transfer, Secondment or Loan of Staff among the Organizations Applying the United Nations Common System of Salaries and Allowances ("the Inter-Organization Agreement"). This was duly registered under the number B-938 by the Treaty Section of the Office of Legal Affairs of the United Nations on 13 June 2003. The purpose of the Inter-Organization Agreement, which is administered by the Chief Executives Board for Coordination of the United Nations, is to facilitate the exchange of staff between the United Nations, its specialized agencies and other intergovernmental organizations applying the United Nations common system of salaries and allowances, by defining the rights and obligations of a staff member being transferred, seconded or loaned from one organization to another and by setting out the rights and liabilities of the two organizations concerned.

The relationship agreement also provides mechanisms for reciprocal representation at meetings, taking into account the status of the Authority as an observer at the United Nations.

The relationship agreement establishes mechanisms whereby the Authority and the United Nations will cooperate in exchanging information and in fulfilling their respective functions under the 1982 Convention. Most importantly, article 12 of the agreement provides that unless the General Assembly, after giving reasonable notice to the Authority, decides otherwise, the United Nations will continue to make available to the Authority, on a cost reimbursable basis, such facilities and services as may be required for the meetings of the Authority, including translation and interpretation services, documentation, and conference services.

A similar Agreement on Cooperation and Relationship between the United Nations and the International Tribunal for the Law of the Sea, establishing a mechanism for cooperation between the two institutions, was signed by the Secretary-General of the United Nations and the President of the International Tribunal for the Law of the Sea on 18 December 1997 in New York. According to its terms, the agreement is to be applied provisionally by the United Nations and the International Tribunal for the Law of the Sea upon signature and will enter into force on its approval by the General Assembly of the United Nations and the International Tribunal for the Law of the Sea. The International Tribunal for the Law of the Sea confirmed its approval of the Agreement on 12 March 1998 at its fifth session. On 8 September 1998, it was approved by resolution adopted by the General Assembly of the United Nations (A/RES/52/251) and entered into force on that day.

DOCUMENTARY SOURCES

- PREPARATORY COMMISSION

LOS/PCN/WP.50/Rev.3, Final draft Agreement concerning the relationship between the United Nations and the International Seabed Authority, reproduced in: LOS/PCN/153, Vol. V, 142-149.

- ISBA

ISBA/A/15, Decision of the Assembly relating to participation of the International Seabed Authority in the United Nations Joint Staff Pension Fund, (*Selected Decisions 1/2/3*, 28-29).

ISBA/A/L.11, Draft decision of the Assembly relating to participation in the United Nations Joint Staff Pension Fund.

ISBA/A/L.13, Statement of the President on the work of the Assembly during the resumed second session, para. 18, (*Selected Decisions 1/2/3*, 32).

ISBA/3/A/3, Decision of the Assembly relating to the Agreement concerning the relationship between the United Nations and the International Seabed Authority, (*Selected Decisions 1/2/3*, 43).

ISBA/3/A/4, Report of the Secretary-General of the International Seabed Authority under article 166, paragraph 4, of the United Nations

Convention on the Law of the Sea, paras. 13 and 20-21, (*Selected Decisions 1/2/3*, 48 and 50).

ISBA/3/A/L.2, Relationship agreement between the United Nations and the International Seabed Authority.

ISBA/3/A/L.4, Statement of the President on the work of the Assembly during the third session, paras. 1 and 10, (*Selected Decisions 1/2/3*, 43 and 45).

ISBA/4/A/11, Report of the Secretary-General of the International Seabed Authority under article 166, paragraph 4, of the United Nations Convention on the Law of the Sea, paras. 13 and 26, (*Selected Decisions 4*, 54).

ISBA/10/A/3, Report of the Secretary-General of the International Seabed Authority under article 166, paragraph 4, of the United Nations Convention on the Law of the Sea, paras. 47, 50 and 53, (*Selected Decisions 10*, 23).

ISBA/C/10, Decision of the Council of the International Seabed Authority concerning the relationship agreement between the International Seabed Authority and the United Nations, (*Selected Decisions 1/2/3*, 36-37).

ISBA/C/L.3, Statement of the President Pro Tem on the work of the Council during the resumed second session, para. 11, (*Selected Decisions 1/2/3*, 39).

ISBA/3/C/4, Recommendation by the Council relating to the relationship agreement between the United Nations and the International Seabed Authority.

ISBA/3/C/L.2, Agreement concerning the relationship between the United Nations and the International Seabed Authority.

ISBA/3/C/L.4, Statement of the President on the work of the Council during the third session, para. 9, (*Selected Decisions 1/2/3*, 65).

ISBA/16/C/4, Amendments to the Staff Regulations of the International Seabed Authority, (*Selected Decisions 16*, 85-90).

ISBA/16/C/14*, Statement of the President of the Council of the International Seabed Authority on the work of the Council during the sixteenth session, para. 15, (*Selected Decisions 16*, 111).

- UNITED NATIONS

A/RES/51/34, Law of the sea.

A/RES/52/27, Agreement concerning the relationship between the United Nations and the International Seabed Authority.

United Nations, *Treaty Series*, vol. 2217, B-938.

RELATIONS WITH OTHER INTERNATIONAL ORGANIZATIONS

MEMORANDUM OF UNDERSTANDING BETWEEN THE INTERGOVERNMENTAL OCEANOGRAPHIC COMMISSION OF UNESCO AND THE INTERNATIONAL SEABED AUTHORITY

The purpose of this Memorandum of Understanding is to specify the scope of co-operation between the Intergovernmental Oceanographic Commission of UNESCO (hereinafter referred to as "the IOC") and the International Seabed Authority (hereinafter referred to as "the Authority") in promoting the development and conduct of marine scientific research in the international seabed area and in publication and dissemination of research and analysis results for the mutual benefit of Member States and in the light of the relevant provisions of the United Nations Convention on the Law of the Sea of 10 December 1982 (hereinafter referred to as "the Convention", notably articles 143, 163 (13), and 169, as well as Section 1 (5) (h) of the Agreement relating to the Implementation of Part XI of the Convention adopted on 28 July 1994 by the United Nations General Assembly, Resolution 48/263 "the Agreement").

THE IOC AND THE AUTHORITY AGREE:

1.   to consult, where appropriate and practical, on issues of mutual interest in the field of marine scientific research, related services and capacity building with a view to promoting or enhancing a better understanding of activities in the international seabed area;

2.   to work in close co-operation, where appropriate and practical, in the field of ocean services, particularly in the collection of environmental data and information. For that purpose, the World Data Centres of the IOC/IODE Programme may assist the Authority to identify the existing gaps, to retrieve appropriate data and to develop a database to be used for analysis and synthesis;

3.   to invite each other's representatives to attend and participate in the meetings of their respective governing bodies as observers in accordance with the rules of procedures of such bodies;

4.   to exchange data and information as appropriate on matters of mutual interest;

5.   to conduct, where appropriate, co-operative studies and seminars;

6.   that this Memorandum of Understanding is without prejudice to agreements concluded by either party with other organizations and programmes;

7.   that the co-operation between the two organizations referred to herein is subject to the requirement of confidentiality of data and information imposed upon the Authority by the Convention in respect of data and information submitted to it by applicants and contractors for exploration of resources of the international seabed area;

8.   that this Memorandum of Understanding will come into effect upon its signature by the Executive Secretary of IOC and the Secretary-General of the International Seabed Authority. It may be terminated by any of the parties by giving to the other a written notice six months prior to the proposed date of termination;

IN WITNESS WHEREOF the undersigned have signed the present Memorandum of Understanding in duplicate.

Patricio BERNAL
Executive Secretary
International Oceanographic Commission
Date: 7 July 2000

Satya N. NANDAN
Secretary-General
International Seabed Authority
Date: 5 May 2000

COMMENTARY

In May 2000, the Secretary-General of the Authority and the Executive Secretary of the Intergovernmental Oceanographic Commission (IOC/UNESCO) signed a Memorandum of Understanding concerning cooperation between the two organizations in promoting the conduct of marine scientific research in the international seabed area. Under the Memorandum of Understanding, the two organizations will, where appropriate and practical, consult on matters of mutual interest in the field of marine scientific research and cooperate in the collection of environmental data and information.

DOCUMENTARY SOURCES

- ISBA

ISBA/6/A/9, Report of the Secretary-General of the International Seabed Authority under article 166, paragraph 4, of the United Nations Convention on the Law of the Sea, para. 13, (*Selected Decisions 6*, 15).

MEMORANDUM OF UNDERSTANDING BETWEEN THE OSPAR COMMISSION AND THE INTERNATIONAL SEABED AUTHORITY

The purpose of this memorandum of understanding is to specify the scope of cooperation between the Commission established by the Convention for the Protection of the Marine Environment of the North-East Atlantic ("OSPAR Convention"), signed in Paris on 22 September 1992 (hereinafter referred to as "the OSPAR Commission") and the International Seabed Authority (hereinafter referred to as "the Authority") established by the United Nations Convention on the Law of the Sea ("the Convention") signed in Montego Bay on 10 December 1982.

WHEREAS:

The OSPAR Commission has been taking initiatives to establish a network of marine protected areas in order to protect biodiversity in areas beyond national jurisdiction, as part of its obligations under the OSPAR Convention and its annex V;

The OSPAR Commission in fulfilling its obligations seeks, where appropriate, to cooperate with competent regional organizations and other competent international organizations and competent bodies;

The OSPAR Commission issued a Code of Conduct for Responsible Marine Research in the Deep Seas and High Seas of the OSPAR Maritime Area;

The Authority is the competent organization through which States Parties to the Convention shall, in accordance with Part XI of the Convention and the 1994 Agreement relating to the Implementation of Part XI of the Convention adopted on 28 July 1994 by the United Nations General Assembly, resolution 48/263 ("the 1994 Agreement"), organize and control activities in the Area, particularly with a view to administering the mineral resources of the Area, as defined in article 1, paragraph 1 (1) of the Convention;

The Authority promotes and encourages the conduct of marine scientific research with respect to activities in the Area and the collection and dissemination of the results of such research and analysis, when available, with particular emphasis on research related to the environmental impact of activities in the Area in accordance with article 143 of the Convention and section 1, paragraph 5 (h) of the 1994 Agreement;

The Authority is competent to take necessary measures in order to ensure effective protection of the marine environment from harmful effects which may arise from activities in the Area as set out in article 145 of the Convention and section 1, paragraph 5 (g) of the 1994 Agreement;

The Authority seeks consultation and cooperation with, *inter alia*, international organizations on matters within the competence of the Authority;

All parties to the OSPAR Convention are members of the Authority;

In areas where the "maritime area" defined in article 1 (a) of the OSPAR Convention and the "Area" defined in article 1, paragraph 1 (1) of the Convention overlap, both the OSPAR Commission and the Authority have complementary competence; this competence to be exercised in accordance with the principles governing the Area as stipulated in section 2 of Part XI of the Convention;

The OSPAR Commission and the Authority both have a strong interest in the protection of the marine environment, including of vulnerable deep sea ecosystems in the Area that are associated with some mineral resources, and have taken initiatives at a regional scale in that respect, respectively in the Charlie Gibbs Fracture Zone on the Mid-Atlantic Ridge and in the Clarion-Clipperton Fracture Zone in the Pacific Ocean;

Increased cooperation between the OSPAR Commission and the Authority will help ensure appropriate coordination of measures in order to conciliate the development of mineral resources with comprehensive protection of the marine environment;

Consultation will help guarantee that marine protected areas are established with due regard to the rights and duties of States and the Authority as set out in the Convention and the 1994 Agreement;

THE OSPAR COMMISSION AND THE AUTHORITY HAVE DECIDED:

1.   To consult, where appropriate and practical, on matters of mutual interest with a view to promoting or enhancing a better understanding and coordination of their respective activities in respect of such matters;

2.   To encourage the conduct of marine scientific research in the sea areas of the North-East Atlantic that are located beyond national jurisdiction, in order to contribute towards ongoing assessments, on the basis of the best available scientific information and in accordance with the precautionary and ecosystem approaches, of:

    (i)   The distribution, abundance and condition of vulnerable deep water habitats;

    (ii) The status of populations of marine species;

    (iii) The effectiveness of measures aimed at the conservation of marine biological diversity in areas beyond national jurisdiction in the North-East Atlantic;

3.   To cooperate, where appropriate and practical, in the collection of environmental data and information and, where possible, to exchange standardized data and information, including reports of meetings of relevance to each other;

4. To invite each other's representatives to attend and participate in the meetings of their respective governing bodies as observers in accordance with the rules of procedure of such bodies, as appropriate;

5. To conduct, where appropriate, cooperative studies and seminars;

6. That this memorandum of understanding is without prejudice to agreements concluded by either signatory with other organizations and programmes;

7. That the cooperation between them is subject to the requirement of confidentiality of data and information imposed upon the Authority by the Convention in respect of data and information submitted to it by applicants and contractors for exploration of resources of the Area;

8. That this memorandum of understanding will come into effect upon its signature by the Chairman of the OSPAR Commission and the Secretary-General of the Authority. It may be terminated by either Signatory by giving six months' written notice to the other signatory, prior to the proposed date of termination;

IN WITNESS WHEREOF, the undersigned have signed the present memorandum of understanding in duplicate.

The Chairman of	The Secretary-General of
the OSPAR Commission	the International Seabed Authority
Date: 20 June 2011	Date: 26 May 2011

COMMENTARY

In 2008, the secretariat of the OSPAR Commission, established by the OSPAR Convention for the Protection of the Marine Environment of the North-East Atlantic,[1] contacted the secretariat of the Authority with respect to a proposal submitted to the OSPAR Commission, for the establishment of a marine protected area at the Charlie Gibbs fracture zone; this area is located beyond the limits of national jurisdiction, but within the OSPAR Convention Area, on the Mid-Atlantic Ridge. In September 2008, an informal meeting took place at secretariat level

---

[1] The mandate of the OSPAR Commission is to supervise the implementation of its constituent instrument. The Contracting Parties to the OSPAR Convention are Belgium, Denmark, the European Union, Finland, France, Germany, Iceland, Ireland, Luxembourg, the Netherlands, Norway, Portugal, Spain, Sweden, Switzerland and the United Kingdom of Great Britain and Northern Ireland. All 16 Contracting Parties to the OSPAR Convention are also members of the Authority.

between the secretariat of the OSPAR Commission, the Authority and the secretariat of the North-East Atlantic Fisheries Commission (NEAFC), when it was agreed that, given the overlapping jurisdictions and mandates of the organizations concerned, and in particular the Authority's mandate with respect to the seabed beyond the limits of national jurisdiction of the OSPAR Convention Area, a dialogue should be established to ensure that marine protected areas are established with due regard to the rights and duties of States as set out in the 1982 Convention and the 1994 Agreement as well as with full respect for the jurisdiction of the Authority to manage activities in the Area. At their meeting held on 11 to 12 November 2008, the OSPAR Heads of Delegation acknowledged the mandate of the Authority as the competent organization to regulate deep seabed mining and supported the idea of developing a memorandum of understanding between the OSPAR Commission and the Authority in order to ensure appropriate coordination of measures between the two organizations.

At the fifteenth session of the Authority in 2009, during the debate on the annual report of the Secretary-General of the Authority, the Assembly welcomed the idea of enhancing the cooperative relationship between the OSPAR Commission and the Authority as a valuable step forward for the Authority. The Assembly also requested the Secretary-General to pursue the dialogue with the Executive Secretary of the OSPAR Commission in order to develop the terms of a memorandum of understanding between the OSPAR Commission and the Authority.

Following further discussions between the secretariats of the two organizations on the terms of a memorandum of understanding, a draft prepared by the Authority was circulated to OSPAR Contracting Parties in accordance with the procedures of the organization; this was further considered at the meeting of the OSPAR Commission heads of delegation on 17 February 2010. Subject to editorial changes, the heads of delegation agreed that the proposed memorandum of understanding should be submitted to the Authority for approval at the sixteenth session.

During the sixteenth session, at its one hundred and twenty-fifth meeting, on 27 April 2010, the Assembly of the Authority took note of the text of the memorandum of understanding (ISBA/16/A/INF/2, Annex) and approved it. The Assembly also considered the request for observer status by the OSPAR Commission and decided to invite it to participate in its meetings in the capacity of observer, pursuant to rule 82, paragraph 1 (d) of the rules of procedure of the Assembly.

Following its approval by the Assembly, the memorandum of understanding was submitted to the OSPAR Commission heads of delegation for approval at the annual meeting of the OSPAR Commission in Bergen, Norway from 20-24 September 2010. The OSPAR Commission approved the MOU and agreed to grant reciprocal observer status to the Authority. The memorandum was signed by the Secretary-General of the Authority and the Chairman of the OSPAR Commission on 26 May 2011 and 20 June 2011, respectively.

DOCUMENTARY SOURCES

- ISBA

ISBA/15/A/2, Report of the Secretary-General of the International Seabed Authority under article 166, paragraph 4, of the United Nations Convention on the Law of the Sea, paras. 19-21, (*Selected Decisions 15*, 4).

ISBA/15/A/9, Statement of the President of the Assembly of the International Seabed Authority on the work of the Assembly at the fifteenth session, para. 13, (*Selected Decisions 15*, 31).

ISBA/16/A/INF.2, Request for observer status in accordance with rule 82, paragraph 1 (d) of the rules of procedure of the Assembly on behalf of the OSPAR Commission.

ISBA/16/A/2, Report of the Secretary-General of the International Seabed Authority under article 166, paragraph 4, of the United Nations Convention on the Law of the Sea, paras. 17-18 and 115, (*Selected Decisions 16*, 3-4 and 25).

ISBA/16/A/13, Statement of the President of the Assembly of the International Seabed Authority on the work of the Assembly at its sixteenth session, para. 6, (*Selected Decisions 16*, 76).

B - RELATIONS WITH NON-GOVERNMENTAL ORGANIZATIONS

MEMORANDUM OF UNDERSTANDING BETWEEN THE INTERNATIONAL CABLE PROTECTION COMMITTEE AND THE INTERNATIONAL SEABED AUTHORITY

The purpose of this memorandum of understanding is to specify the scope of cooperation between the International Cable Protection Committee Ltd (hereinafter referred to as "the ICPC") and the International Seabed Authority (hereinafter referred to as "the Authority").

WHEREAS:

The ICPC is an organization representing the submarine cable industry that has been established to promote the security and safeguarding of submarine cables against man-made and natural hazards;

Submarine cables provide critical infrastructure, and the laying of submarine cables is one of the freedoms of the high seas under articles 87 and 112 to 115 of the United Nations Convention on the Law of the Sea of 10 December 1982 ("the Convention"), which freedoms shall be exercised by all States with due regard for the interests of other States and for the rights under the Convention with respect to activities in the Area, defined in article 1, paragraph 1 (1), of the Convention as the seabed and ocean floor and subsoil thereof, beyond the limits of national jurisdiction;

The Authority is the organization through which States parties to the Convention shall, in accordance with Part XI of the Convention and the Agreement relating to the implementation of Part XI of the Convention adopted on 28 July 1994 by the United Nations General Assembly in its resolution 48/263 ("the Agreement"), organize and control activities in the Area, particularly with a view to administering the mineral resources of the Area;

Both the ICPC and the Authority have a strong interest in the protection of the marine environment from harmful effects arising from their respective activities;

Increased cooperation between the ICPC and the Authority would help to avoid potential conflicts between the laying and maintaining of submarine cables and current and future activities in the Area;

THE ICPC AND THE AUTHORITY THEREFORE AGREE:

1.   To consult, where appropriate and practical, on issues of mutual interest, with a view to promoting or enhancing a better understanding of their respective activities;

2.   To invite each other's representatives to attend and participate in the meetings of their respective governing bodies as observers in accordance with the rules of procedures of such bodies;

3.   To exchange where practicable, or to facilitate by direct liaison with the owners of international cable systems, information on cable routings and prospecting and exploration areas, subject to confidentiality provisions;

4.   To cooperate, where appropriate and practical, in the collection of environmental data and information and, where possible, to exchange standardized data and information;

5.   To conduct, where appropriate, cooperative studies and seminars;

6.   To invite each other's representatives to participate in relevant meetings of experts and workshops;

7.   That this memorandum of understanding is without prejudice to agreements concluded by either party with other organizations and programmes;

8.   That the cooperation between the two organizations referred to herein is subject to the requirements of confidentiality of data and information imposed upon the Authority by the Convention, the Agreement and the relevant rules, regulations and procedures of the Authority in respect of data and information submitted to it by applicants and contractors for exploration and exploitation in the Area and upon the ICPC in accordance with its rules, articles and member approval as provided therein;

9.   That this memorandum of understanding will come into effect upon its signature by the Chairman of the ICPC and the Secretary-General of the Authority. It may be terminated by any of the parties by giving to the other a written notice six months prior to the proposed date of termination.

IN WITNESS WHEREOF, the undersigned have signed the present memorandum of understanding in duplicate.

(Signed)	(Signed)
Chairman of the International Cable	Secretary-General of the
Protection Committee	International Seabed Authority
25 February 2010	15 December 2009

COMMENTARY

The International Cable Protection Committee (ICPC) is the global organization representing the telecommunications and cable-laying industry. Established in 1958, the ICPC is mandated to provide leadership and guidance on issues related to the planning, installation, operation, maintenance and protection of submarine cables against man-made and natural hazards. It also provides a forum for the exchange of technical and legal information pertaining to submarine cable protection methods and programmes, including exchanging information on the location of existing and proposed cables.

During the fifteenth session of the Authority in 2009, following the practice of arranging technical briefings for the representatives of members of the Authority present in Kingston on matters relevant to the work of the Council and the Assembly, the Council was given a briefing on the work of ICPC by its Chairman. In discussions thereafter, members of the Authority noted that, while the laying of submarine cables is a freedom of the high seas, it was in the interests of both the Authority and the members of ICPC to cooperate to avoid potential conflicts between the laying of cables and activities in the Area. It was further noted that both organizations also had a strong interest in the protection of the marine environment from adverse impacts arising from their respective activities. It was therefore suggested that ICPC should be invited to become an observer to the Assembly in accordance with rule 82, paragraph 1 (e), of the rules of procedure of the Assembly.

Following further discussions between the secretariat of the Authority and ICPC, it was considered desirable to conclude a memorandum of understanding setting out the scope and purpose of cooperation between the two organizations. The memorandum was signed by the Secretary-General of the Authority and the Chairman of ICPC on 15 December 2009 and 25 February 2010, respectively.

The memorandum, together with the request for observer status by the ICPC, was submitted to the Assembly for approval during the sixteenth session. At its one hundred and twenty-fifth meeting, on 27 April 2010, the Assembly decided to invite ICPC to participate in the Assembly in the capacity of observer, pursuant to rule 82, paragraph 1 (e), of the rules of procedure of the Assembly. The Assembly also took note of the memorandum of understanding signed between ICPC and the Authority (ISBA/16/A/INF/1, Annex) and approved it.

DOCUMENTARY SOURCES

- ISBA

ISBA/15/A/2, Report of the Secretary-General of the International Seabed
Authority under article 166, paragraph 4, of the United Nations
Convention on the Law of the Sea, para. 22, (*Selected Decisions 15*, 5).

ISBA/15/A/9, Statement of the President of the Assembly of the
International Seabed Authority on the work of the Assembly at the
fifteenth session, para. 13, (*Selected Decisions 15*, 31).

ISBA/16/A/INF.1, Request for observer status in accordance with rule
82, paragraph 1 (e), of the rules of procedure of the Assembly on
behalf of the International Cable Protection Committee.

ISBA/16/A/2, Report of the Secretary-General of the International
Seabed Authority under article 166, paragraph 4, of the United
Nations Convention on the Law of the Sea, paras. 19-21, (*Selected
Decisions 16*, 4).

ISBA/16/A/13, Statement of the President of the Assembly of the
International Seabed Authority on the work of the Assembly at its
sixteenth session, para. 6, (*Selected Decisions 16*, 76).